Ray Billows

The Cinderella Kid

Ray Billows

The Cinderella Kid

The unlikely and colorful story
of a world-class amateur golfer

Tom Buggy

© Copyright, Tom Buggy 2016

Photo Credits
Front Cover, First Title Page: USGA Photo Archives
1935 New York State Amateur: USGA Photo Archives
1938 Walker Cup Team: USGA Photo Archives
1949 Walker Cup Team: USGA Photo Archives
Family, Ray with Pipe, At Rhoads Hospital: Barbara Tilles
Byron Nelson Exhibition, 1953 Portrait: Barbara Tilles
All other photographs: Tom Buggy

ISBN: 978-1-0880-3247-3

All rights reserved. No part of this publication may be reproduced, stored in a retrieval system, or transmitted in any form or by any means, electronic, mechanical, photocopying, recording or otherwise, without prior permission of the copyright holder.

Printed in the United States of America

For my wife Jackie, with thanks for her lifetime patience with a dreamer, and for Ray's daughter Barbara, with thanks for allowing me to share a reunion with her father.

"Well, I know I'm the only guy to have reached the final three times and lost each time, but I'd rather be remembered as someone who gave his best. Because I always did."

— Ray Billows

"I can also say with all my heart that I think it's a rotten shame for us so readily to overlook the fine fellows and the truly great golfers who for one reason or another never have got within that charmed circle of national championship."

— Bobby Jones

CONTENTS

Prologue		1
1	Beginnings in Wisconsin	3
2	The Cinderella Kid is Born	7
3	Going National	13
4	A Jam-packed Year	17
5	Getting to the Finals	23
6	The Walker Cup and a Duke	33
7	The Masters, the U.S. Amateur and a Strawberry Blonde	41
8	The Wrong Time to Get Sick	51
9	A Change of Mind	59
10	War Years	65
11	Back in Full Swing	71
12	Third Time a Charm - ?	75
13	Changes in the 1950s	83
14	Winding Down	87
15	Final Years	91
Epilogue		93
Appendix		97
Acknowledgements		107
About the Author		109
Index		111

Prologue

When Bob Jones completed the Grand Slam at Merion Golf Club in 1930 a transition was underway in the game of golf. Jones' accomplishment, which was called the Grand Slam by O.B. Keeler and the Impregnable Quadrilateral by sportswriter George Trevor, and which has never been equaled, consisted of winning the Open and Amateur championships of the United States and Great Britain in the same year. It was then, and remains now, the supreme accomplishment by amateur golfers, who had dominated the game of golf from its beginnings.

By 1930, despite the overwhelming presence of Jones, professional golfers had begun to challenge the amateurs for the attention of the American golfing public. Professionals such as Walter Hagen and Gene Sarazen had led the way. By the 1940s names like Hogan, Nelson and Snead attracted the public eye; they were followed by Palmer, Nicklaus, Watson and others until professional golf dominated the scene. The retirement of Jones accelerated the transition.

In the interim, a band of amateurs continued to capture the public's interest into the 1950s. Johnny Goodman, Marvin "Bud" Ward, Lawson Little, Johnny Fischer, Willie Turnesa, Frank Stranahan, Charlie Yates and others, drew public attention and large crowds to amateur championships, especially the U.S. Amateur and the Walker Cup.

In the year Bob Jones won his Grand Slam, a teenager from a struggling family in Racine, Wisconsin discovered the game of golf. He set about on his own to join this band of amateurs and reach the highest levels of amateur golf. While doing so he established a reputation as one of golf's most colorful characters, and one of the most humble and finest gentlemen in the game.

His name is Ray Billows. He was called the Cinderella Kid. This is his story.

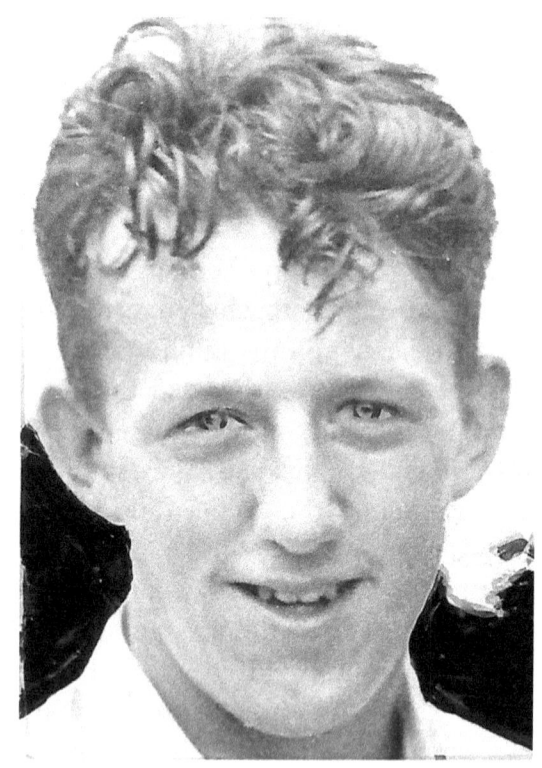

Ray at Age 21

1 Beginnings in Wisconsin

Sometime between the years 1900 and 1910, George W. Billow left his family's home in Hunters Valley, Pennsylvania near Harrisburg and arrived in Fond du Lac, Wisconsin. The reason for his relocation was most likely the prospect of employment. His last known occupation in Pennsylvania was as a day laborer.

George gained a job as a machinist at the Harris Typewriter Works in the small Wisconsin town at the southern end of Lake Winnebago (Fond du Lac means "foot of the lake"). On June 12, 1913 he married Fond du Lac resident Clara Trier. A newspaper report of the wedding mentioned that Clara carried an amethyst rosary, an observation that reflected her strong devotion to the Catholic religion. That devotion would have a lasting impact on a future son.

On June 12, 1914, Clara gave birth to the couple's first child, a son who was given the name of Raymond Edward Billow. (How Billow became Billows will be explained in a later chapter.) Ray was joined in the family by his sister Marie in 1918. In 1920 the family moved to Racine, Wisconsin, apparently to take advantage of an employment opportunity for George. In the 1930 U.S. Census he is listed as a metal worker in the auto industry. Ray entered high school at Washington Park High School and began to play golf seriously in 1930. It is not known what led him to the game. Could it have been the influence of the Grand Slam by Bob Jones? Was the opportunity to earn money as a caddie a factor? It could have been both. As Ray continued to demonstrate in later years, he approached the game with great enthusiasm, tenacity and self-reliance.

Much of Ray's early golf was played at the Washington Park Golf Course in Racine, a modest nine-hole public course that is the oldest golf course on record still within the city limits of any city in the state of Wisconsin. His game developed quickly and was completely self-taught – he claimed never to have taken a golf lesson during the fifty years of his active golf life. The extent and speed of his development were remarkable. In September, 1931 at age 17 he was the low amateur in the Wisconsin Open tournament.

At Racine Country Club Ray met a fellow caddie who would become a high school teammate, friend and competitor. His name was Wilford Wehrle who, like Ray, would become a nationally ranked amateur golfer and a member of the Wisconsin Golf Association Hall of Fame. Together they formed the nucleus of a powerful high school golf team. In 1931 they led their Washington Park High School team to a first-place finish in the state tournament, and Wehrle won the individual title. In 1932, the team finished third; Ray won Medalist honors in the qualifying round and finished second by one stroke in the 36-hole individual championship after an even-par final round.

Ray's high school performance on the golf course wasn't always matched by performance in the classroom. Actually, Ray wasn't in the classroom as much as he should have been. He was a truant who skipped school frequently to play golf, caddie or just search for lost golf balls at Racine Country Club. As his daughter Barbara recalls, "Ray got into a little trouble in high school. He was a cocky young guy. I don't know what might have happened to him if it wasn't for golf." However, Ray graduated from high school and he is also a member of the Washington Park High School Hall of Fame.

What happened to Ray from 1933 to 1935 was a whirlwind of success on the golf course and a caddying experience that shaped the rest of his life. He won three consecutive Racine County Amateur championships during this period.

In 1934 Ray also won the Milwaukee District Championship, reached the semifinals of the State Amateur, was the third leading amateur in the Western Open, finished fourth in the State Open, and set a course record of 65 at the Washington Park course. In 1935 he was ranked as the #2 amateur in Wisconsin and finished second in the State Open to professional Johnny Revolta, who was a national PGA champion.

At the end of 1934, flushed with success, Ray gave serious thought to becoming a professional golfer. A September article in the *Milwaukee Journal* reported Ray as saying: "I've worked hard on my game, practicing all summer, and I feel that by continuing to apply myself I could make a success as a pro. At least I'd like to have a shot at it." It didn't happen. But why didn't it happen? One reason may have been the realization that the life of a golf professional wasn't anywhere near as glamorous or financially rewarding as it might have seemed to a twenty-year-old young man. At the time there was nothing like the professional tour of today. Most professionals had mundane club jobs from which they took welcome breaks to compete in tournaments, and the tournament purses were meager. For example, Walter Hagen, one of the leading professionals of the time, had been a club pro at the Country Club of Rochester in New York. The winner of the 1934 U.S. Open received $1,000 and only twenty players won money; the 20th received $20. It wasn't until 1946 that first place money was increased to $1,500 and the prize list extended to thirty players, the last of whom received $100.

Another reason may have been the difficulty for a young amateur golfer with mostly local and area success to secure a job as a professional, or even a job as an assistant professional. But the most likely reason was an unlikely relationship between a caddie and a member of Racine Country Club.

Ray had continued to caddie during the early 1930s. Traveling to and playing in amateur tournaments required money that was in short supply during the years of the Great Depression. In 1934 one of his caddie loops at Racine Country Club was Edward Wadewitz, president of the Whitman Publishing Company, which was headquartered in Racine. Ray promoted himself to Wadewitz as someone who could help his company as an employee. Apparently, Wadewitz liked the initiative of the young caddie and perhaps saw an advantage in having a golf champion as an employee.

Eventually, Edward Wadewitz offered Ray a job as a shipping clerk in a new Western Printing plant that had been established in Poughkeepsie, New York. Ray accepted this tangible opportunity for income instead of the uncertain prospect of becoming a golf professional. So, in late 1934 Ray Billow set out for Poughkeepsie for the start of his new $17-a-week job.

In a 1993 interview Ray recounted how the relationship with Edward Wadewitz had started. "I made a deal with another caddie. I told him I would give him 50 cents if he let me carry for his man." The deal, another example of Ray's initiative and self-reliance, was accepted and, as they say, "The rest is history."

There was one more important happening during Ray's time in Wisconsin. In 1933 his mother Clara died prematurely at age 47. Her death had a profound effect on him. On her deathbed the devout Catholic woman solicited a promise from Ray that he would always attend Sunday Mass. It was a promise he kept for the rest of his life.

The Cinderella Kid

2   The Cinderella Kid is Born

Had there been background music when the 1935 golf season got underway in the Poughkeepsie area, it may well have been a precursor of the 1970s Eagles song *New Kid in Town*. The headline of an April 6 article in the *Poughkeepsie Eagle-News* blared out: "Local Golfers Take Heed! Newcomer Threatens Titles."

The article went on to say that Ray Billows – suddenly it was Billows instead of Billow – walked onto the Dutchess Golf and Country Club course and shot even-par 35 for nine holes, and that he had also toured the nine-hole Millbrook Country Club course in 28 strokes on temporary greens. Ray was described as being five feet, ten inches tall and weighing 156 pounds. It was noted that he intended to continue his quest for a big title in top tournaments and that he planned to join the Dutchess club on the following weekend.

The first "top tournament" on the horizon was the New York State Amateur, which was to be conducted by the New York State Golf Association (NYSGA) in July. An entry requirement was that a participant had to be a member of a NYSGA golf club. There has long been a question about how Ray met the requirement. One version says that he "arranged" to become a club member in order to play in the tournament. The other version is that he actually joined Dutchess. A June 27, 1935 newspaper article settles the question; he joined Dutchess in the spring of that year.

In the interim to the New York State Amateur tournament, Ray settled into his $17-a-week job at Western Printing preparing invoices and managing other shipping tasks. He also purchased a car, a well worn Ford Model 'T' convertible coupe that came to be known as the "flivver," a term synonymous with "jalopy," "junker," "wreck," etc. The purchase price of $7 reflected both the car's affordability for Ray and its sorry condition. *New York Sun* sportswriter George Trevor described the flivver well:

The Billows car is the only one of its kind in America. Its paintless body of the once familiar bathtub type suggests the rust-sheathed hull of a dry-docked steamer; its fenders are chewed to ribbons; the upholstery has long since burst at every seam, allowing stuffing to stream out like ectoplasm from a spiritual medium. The tires, liberally plastered with blowout patches, are down to a canvas. But, regardless of all this, Billows is a grand golfer and one of the finest kids in America.

The site of the tournament was the prestigious Winged Foot Golf Club in Mamaroneck. Ray drove the flivver to Winged Foot. When he arrived in the club parking lot the car stalled, which was the least of his problems. He was confronted by club members who threatened to evict both him and the car from the premises. When he explained that he was a tournament participant and not a caddie, and that he intended to sleep next to the car during the tournament, he received the predictable response – not acceptable!

Sympathy and generosity then entered the scene. Depending on which newspaper account you read, Ray slept the first night on a clubhouse porch, on a cot in the locker room, or on the locker room floor. Word about the situation made its way to a group of reporters who were covering the tournament. Nan O'Reilly, then the only female sports reporter in New York City, approached Winged Foot members Ed Chapman and Ed Thorp with the plea "How about staking this kid?" The two men did not hesitate. Ray was offered a room and meals in the clubhouse. When it was revealed that he did not have golf shoes with cleats or a sufficient supply of golf clothes, arrangements were made to acquire both from club members. The flivver was relegated to a dark corner of the parking lot.

One final problem confronted Ray. He intended to carry his own golf bag throughout the tournament but was told that was unacceptable at Winged Foot. He informed his assigned caddie that he did not have money to pay him. The caddie's response was: "Mr. Billows, nobody is forcing me to carry your bag. I want to caddie for you." Shades of Eddie Lowery and Francis Ouimet at the historic 1913 U.S. Open! Ray returned to Winged Foot two years later and gave the caddie $100.

With his flivver, clothes and caddie problems behind him, Ray was ready for play. He was, of course, an unknown in New York golf and a decided underdog in the tournament. He scored a 75 in the qualifying round to easily reach the match play portion of the tournament, where he was to meet players of financial and social standing in stark contrast to his own humble standing, and skilled players with very strong records of accomplishment. His first opponent was Charles Pettijohn Jr., a 17-year-old who was about to enter Georgetown University and who in his later years would move to Hollywood as a writer and production manager. He would also author a book titled *Diary of a Rich Man's Kid*. An accomplished young player, Pettijohn got off to a torrid start in the match. He was three under par on the front nine and got to four under when he hit his tee shot on the difficult 200-yard tenth hole a foot from the cup. Ray stayed within reach with his own solid play. When Pettijohn wilted on the remainder of the back nine, Ray's par 36 enabled him to win the match, 2&1.

Next up was George Voigt, the 1928 Long Island Amateur champion and a member of the 1930 and 1932 Walker Cup teams. Ray was 1-Down after ten holes but then won four consecutive holes with two birdies and two pars. Voigt, one of the tournament favorites, battled back but Ray held on to win the match, 1-Up. He had now reached the quarterfinals and a buzz about him was circulating around Winged Foot. News about the flivver, his borrowed clothes and his two unexpected wins aroused curiosity about the newcomer from Wisconsin.

The background of Ray's quarterfinal opponent could not have been further from his own. T. Suffern (Tommy) Tailer was from a family long associated with the financial and social life of New York and the east. He had attended Princeton and was labeled as the "millionaire society golfer." He was also a very good player and the reigning Metropolitan Amateur champion. In 1938 he became the first amateur to score under 70 in the Masters Tournament. With outstanding play Ray won the match 6&5, one of the worst defeats Tailer ever suffered.

In the semifinals Ray met a young man who he would meet several times in future state and national tournaments. One of those times would be in the finals of the U.S. Amateur. The two would also be teammates on a Walker Cup team and become good friends. His opponent was Willie Turnesa, a New Yorker from Westchester County who was one of seven golfing brothers in a humble Italian immigrant family. Six of the brothers became golf professionals, some PGA tournament competitors, some club pros. Willie Turnesa remained a lifetime amateur.

Willie was the co-leader in the qualifying round of the tournament, having shot a one-under-par 71 on the difficult Winged Foot West Course. Considered the finest shotmaker in the tournament and on his way to a future nickname of "Willie the Wedge," he was also a clear favorite to defeat Ray. Their match was a close and spirited one. Ray never trailed, but he never led by more than two holes. The match was all-square after nine holes. Ray won the tenth and eleventh holes to go 2-Up and maintained that margin through the fourteenth hole. Willie battled back to win the next two holes. The final two holes were halved, which forced a sudden death playoff. Ray won the match with a par 4 on the nineteenth hole.

The stage was now set for an unexpected final match. Ray's opponent was 19-year-old Jack Creavy from Albany, New York, who was the reigning New York State Junior Champion and the kid brother of professional and PGA Champion Tom Creavy. Jack had easily defeated well-known amateur and Winged Foot member Dick Chapman 5&4 in his semifinal match.

The 36-hole final was thrilling and wasn't settled until a 37th hole was played. It also had one of what turned out to be many dogged comebacks by Ray over his career. Actually, there were three comebacks by him in this one match. Creavy built a 2-Up lead after just four holes but Ray battled back to square the match after the first nine. Creavy built another 2-Up lead by the twelfth hole; again, Ray was able to fight back and ended the morning round just one hole behind.

Creavy quickly built his lead to four holes by winning the 20th, 21st and 22nd holes and still had that margin after the 28th hole. A beaten golfer in the estimation of everyone but himself after he came off the 28th green, Ray rose to the occasion as few had done before him. Although Creavy played the last eight holes in only two over par, Ray made up his four-hole deficit, squared the match on the 35th hole after winning the 34th with a spectacular eagle, and saved it by playing a marvelous chip shot to save par on the 36th.

Tension filled the air as the players approached the first (37th) green. Both had missed the green in regulation. Creavy played his third shot to forty feet above the hole; Ray was left with a 10-foot putt. Creavy almost holed his putt; he left his ball within an inch of the hole and squarely in the line of Ray's putt – a so-called stymie that was part of the game at the time. It seemed impossible for Ray to hole his ball without touching Creavy's, but with deadly accuracy he sent his ball narrowly past the Creavy ball and into the hole for a winning four.

Ray Billows, a ragamuffin $17-a-week shipping clerk had won the biggest title of his young life. He was carried to the Winged Foot clubhouse on the shoulders of some three score of caddies who had made him their idol. Like them, he had little money; like them, he was one of the ordinary people; as they hoped to do, he had fulfilled a dream, and he had done so with grit and an iron will which they respected greatly.

The press was just as enthusiastic as the caddies about what they had seen; they couldn't resist posing Ray with the large championship trophy and the flivver, which together seemed to capture all that he was. The result was one of golf's iconic photographs – Ray sitting atop the flivver, trophy in hand, with an enthusiastic crowd all around.

Ray Billows was about to leave Winged Foot as a champion and, courtesy of sportswriter Trevor, with a nickname that captured him and what he had accomplished. The nickname would stay with him for his entire golf career:

"The Cinderella Kid"

Except that Ray couldn't leave. Someone had stolen the keys to the flivver. After crossing a few wires, Ray set out for

Poughkeepsie, only to encounter more problems along the way, a stalled flivver and a tire blowout in White Plains. License plates were removed and the car was pushed into a nearby field. Ray finished the trip home in the car of one of the many Dutchess club members who had made the trip to Winged Foot to watch the final round.

Ray considered abandoning the car but he just couldn't do it. The following day, Sunday, after spending $5.40 for a new tire and tube, and attending Mass, he returned to retrieve his cherished car. He was back at work at his shipping clerk's desk on Monday morning.

****

About that name change from Billow to Billows, there are two versions of how it came about. One version says that Ray's high school classmates in Racine started to call him Billows. The other version attributes the change to the report of Ray's arrival in Poughkeepsie in the *Poughkeepsie Eagle-News*. Both versions may be true but the second version is more likely. The Racine newspapers were using Billow in late 1934, and even in August, 1935 when Ray returned for a visit.

Ray's father George continued to use the Billow name when he moved to Poughkeepsie. However, as his son's notoriety grew, he became resigned to the situation and eventually changed his name to Billows. His frustrated comment was "I give up."

3   Going National

When Ray returned to Poughkeepsie on the July Saturday night of his triumph in the New York State Amateur, he was greeted at his Dutchess Golf and Country Club by an enthusiastic crowd of well-wishers. Club members, beaming with pride for having the club's first state champion, couldn't congratulate him, or thank him, enough. But there were questions as well. What were his plans? What tournaments was he going to play in? Was he going to turn pro? And, most especially, was he going to try to qualify for the U.S. Amateur in Cleveland?

Ray accepted the congratulations in the shy, quiet and humble way that characterized him. As for the questions, no, he wasn't going to turn pro – "I'm happy the way I am now." As for his tournament plans, they would depend on what time off he could work out with the Western Printing Company. He said that he'd love to play in the Amateur but he had already used much of his company vacation time.

Ray may not have been sure of his plans but the Dutchess club members were sure about theirs. There would be a dinner to celebrate Ray and the state championship. The event would take place on the following Saturday and it would include an exhibition match: Ray and a club member versus his state final opponent Jack Creavy and a friend. There would also be a "crime" committed and a surprise for Ray.

A few days later, Ray returned from a round of golf at the club and discovered that his car was missing from the parking lot. After a fruitless search for the beloved flivver, he reported the theft to the Poughkeepsie police. The car was still missing when Saturday arrived and the exhibition match got underway. As the players stood on the 18th tee, there appeared to be a commotion at the other end of the fairway.

The commotion turned out to be the flivver being driven down the fairway by a couple of club members accompanied by a policeman. When the contingent reached the tee area the policeman asked Ray if the car was his. Ray said it was but he hardly recognized it. It had been refurbished with new upholstery, new tires, a new horn, new lights, and new brakes. It also had a few less dents and a bit of fresh paint. When the policeman asked what he should do with the member who was driving the car, Ray's laughingly reply was "Put him in the coop."

When the laughing stopped Ray was presented with a beautiful wristwatch that was engraved with recognition of his state championship. He said "It is all very fine and I am very grateful." He reported that he had worked things out at his job with respect to the U.S. Amateur and that "the only thing I have to do now is qualify, for I am certain the flivver will be able to stand the long trip to Cleveland."

Ray did qualify for his first U.S. Amateur. He finished fifth in district qualifying on the Lakeville and Deepdale courses on Long Island, New York with rounds of 75-74-149. He was going to Cleveland, but the flivver was not. He decided to travel by train. As it turned out, he traveled to Racine for a job training assignment that would keep him in Wisconsin until December. The assignment allowed him to play in two Wisconsin tournaments on a very compressed schedule.

Ray arrived in Racine on Saturday, August 24, just in time to play in the Racine County Amateur the next day. He won the tournament for the third consecutive year. He was then off to the Kenosha Country Club for the Wisconsin Open on Monday and Tuesday. He finished second to Johnny Revolta, a professional who was a national PGA champion. Ray had won two tournaments in three days, which, together with what he had accomplished in New York and would accomplish in Cleveland, would make him the #2 ranked amateur in Wisconsin.

The 1935 U.S. Amateur was held at The Country Club outside of Cleveland beginning on September 9. Ray won his first two matches handily, 6&4 over W.K. Wolcott and 5&4 over Russell Martin. He was eliminated in the third round on the 19th hole by Fred Haas Jr., a 19-year-old LSU student who would be a future Walker Cup teammate, professional golfer, 5-time PGA Tour winner and a Ryder Cup team member.

The match with Haas was quite a battle, with both players scoring one-over-par 73s. Ray never led but he was never more than one hole behind except after the 13th where Haas birdied for a 2-Up lead. Displaying the comeback ability that would become one of his trademarks, Ray got that hole back on the 14th with a par and evened the match with a birdie on the 16th. After Haas birdied the 17th to regain the lead, Ray evened the match again with a 20-foot putt for a par on the 18th. On the extra hole Ray drove into the rough and his second was just off the green. It took him three to get down from there and Haas won the match with two putts from ten feet for a par.

Ray returned to Racine after the Amateur to complete his training assignment. He took with him something it is doubtful he had planned on – a new car. How it came about isn't known but he now owned a 1934 convertible coupe. The make and model are unknown, but the 1934 model year represented a major upgrade from the flivver, which had once been described by the Poughkeepsie police as "black where not rusty." Ray said that he planned to give the flivver to a friend.

When Ray completed his training assignment and returned to Poughkeepsie in December, he had to be pleased with what he had accomplished in 1935. He had won his first major title with the New York State Amateur, added to his reputation in Wisconsin by winning his third consecutive Racine County Amateur and finishing second in the Wisconsin Open, won the Hudson River Golf Association championship, finished third among the amateurs in the Metropolitan Golf Association Open, and was the first one to break the par of 70 at his home Dutchess Golf and Country Club course, which became an 18-hole course in 1925 and is the only course that has hosted all of the New York State Golf Association championships.

Most importantly, Ray had earned a place on the national golf stage by reaching the third round of the U.S. Amateur. Plus, his training assignment in Racine offered him the prospect of a better job. He had some important family plans as well. Ray Billows was very much looking forward to the coming year.

1935 Met Open – Sleeping with the Flivver

4   A Jam-packed Year

For Ray Billows, 1936 would turn out to be a busier year than he could have imagined. An expanded golf schedule, new job responsibilities and a family move all contributed.

The training assignment in Racine had indeed led to new job responsibilities; Ray was now a print salesman for the Western Printing company. It was a position that he would hold for the remainder of his business career, and one that would lead to regional sales manager responsibilities that would compete with golf for his time. He spent the cold Poughkeepsie winter establishing himself in his new job and relaxing in a different sport – bowling, a sport in which his father excelled. Ray had shown some interest in bowling as a teenager in Racine. He was now a member of a team in a company league, and he was pretty good at the game. Over the years he had an average as high as 180, rolled a 278 game, and had several 600 series.

In April, Ray's father George and his sister Marie moved from Racine and joined him in his Poughkeepsie home. Both of them obtained jobs at Western Printing, undoubtedly with Ray's influence. In June, George married Helen Mahnke, a Racine woman he had met there some time after the death of his first wife Clara in 1933. Marie, who had started to play golf in Racine in 1934, eventually joined the Dutchess Golf and Country Club and became a very active golfer there. She married fellow club member John Sewell in 1940. After John's death in 1972 she married IBM executive Lawrence "Spud" Bailey.

The move of the family members put to rest a rumor that Ray would remain in Wisconsin after his extended stay. He assured the locals: "I will not go west. Poughkeepsie is to be my home from now on."

Ray's golf year began at the Metropolitan Open in May at the exclusive Quaker Ridge Golf Club, just down the road from Winged Foot in Scarsdale, New York. The Quaker Ridge golf course, completed by golden age architect A.W. Tillinghast and often called "Tillie's Treasure," is considered by some to be the

17

best course in the New York metropolitan area. The Metropolitan Golf Association (the Met), which conducts both Open and Amateur Championships among several other tournaments, is noted for the quality of the amateur and professional players at its member clubs.

Ray was the low amateur in the 1936 Met Open, by one stroke over famous amateur Jess Sweetser (more about Jess later) and Jack Creavy, who Ray defeated in the New York State Amateur final the year before. Ray tied for 12th overall. As testament to the quality of the player field, the tournament was won by future hall of famer Byron Nelson. Among the others in the top eleven were Gene Sarazen, Paul Runyan, Henry Picard and Craig Wood.

In June Ray played in his first U.S Open at the Baltusrol Golf Club in Springfield, New Jersey. In May he was one of three amateurs to qualify at the Inwood Country Club on Long Island. His qualifying score was 153. At Baltusrol he shot the same score and missed the 36-hole cut by two strokes.

Later in June the Metropolitan Amateur was played at the original Lido Golf Club on Long Island. The Lido course, which no longer exists, was an engineering marvel. Two million cubic yards of sand were pumped from Reynolds Channel to create the course out of barren marshland. The course was also famous for its architects. It was designed by C.B. Macdonald and Seth Raynor, with a contribution from Alister MacKenzie. Its 18th hole was inspired by MacKenzie's entry in a design competition. A sportswriter claimed that Lido was "the finest course in the world."

Ray reached the tournament final to play George Dunlap Jr. over 36 holes. Dunlap was a well-known veteran amateur who had won the 1933 U.S. Amateur against a field that included Johnny Goodman, who won the U.S. Open earlier in the month, Lawson Little, Chick Evans, Charlie Yates, Johnny Fischer and Willie Turnesa. A match that featured some brilliant golf by Dunlap and a comeback by Ray from 4-Down was decided on the final hole. With the match all-square Ray drove into the rough, hit an excellent recovery shot to avoid a series of bunkers, and dropped his third shot twelve feet from the hole. Dunlap used a brassie (aka a 2-wood) to reach the green in two shots and was left with a 7-foot putt for a birdie. When Ray missed his putt he extended his hand and conceded the match.

Winning the Met Amateur became one of Ray's priorities. It was the major amateur tournament in his home region and one he yearned to win. He played well in it over the years; he still holds the record for the most matches won in the event (53), but it took him until 1948 to collect his only win.

June ended with a disappointment. Ray was eliminated from the Hudson River Golf Association (HRGA) championship in the second round after he had been the low qualifier. The HRGA was founded in 1902 with nine golf clubs in cities along the Hudson River, including the Dutchess club. It grew to include clubs from Yonkers in the south to Columbia County in the north. The association remains active today with individual and team championships and several Days of Golf throughout the year. Ray won the individual championship in 1935, the first of six that he would win over the years.

The 1936 New York State Amateur was held in mid-July at the Bellevue Country Club in Syracuse. Ray was the defending champion. After relatively easy early-round wins, Ray bested Dudley Ward in the quarterfinals, 3&1, after rallying from 2-Down, and Jack Tucker in the semifinals, 2&1. His opponent in the final was Tommy Goodwin, a talented young player from Winged Foot. *New York Times* writer William Richardson's account of the match called it "as thrilling a title match as was ever played." The medal score of both players was even-par 140 for the 36 holes. With a gallery of 2,000 watching, Ray was 2-Up after the first 18 holes. Goodwin never led until the 28th hole. With the match all-square after the 33rd hole, both players were in greenside bunkers on the 34th. Goodwin blasted out to one foot from the hole. When Ray's putt for par missed, Goodwin went 1-Up and held that margin to win the title. It was the first of four runner-up finishes for Ray in the state amateur.

The month of July was also marked by competition in Ray's home area, both in Westchester County and Poughkeepsie. He won the Sweetser Victory Cup at the St. Andrew's Golf Club in Ardsley-on-Hudson by nine shots with a score of 289 that included

19

a hole in one. It was the first of five wins he would have in the tournament that is named after Jess Sweetser, an outstanding amateur of the 1920s and beyond. Jess won the NCAA championship in 1920 and the U.S. Amateur in 1922. In 1926 he became the first American-born player to win the British Amateur. He played on six Walker Cup teams and captained two others; all of the teams were victorious. The Sweetser Victory Cup continues today in a better-ball format.

The inaugural Dutchess County Amateur was held at the College Hill Golf Course, a municipal course in Poughkeepsie that was built as a work relief project of the Great Depression. The course opened in 1933 as the first public-play course in the city. Ray won the championship with a 4&3 win over Joe Vallo of Beacon, New York in the 36-hole final. The match was all-square after 18 holes. Ray started the second 18 with an eagle on the par-4 first hole (he drove the green) and followed it with a par and birdie to pull away.

During July Ray broke the course record at the Dutchess club with a score of 66 (he had tied the record of 67 in June). After not competing in 1935 because of a conflict with the state amateur tournament, he won his first Dutchess Golf and Country Club championship by defeating University of Pennsylvania golf captain Jim Peelor 7&6 in the 36-hole final. It was the first of four consecutive wins in the tournament, and the first of his 14 club championships, a record that remains intact today.

All that now remained on a jam-packed 1936 schedule was the U.S. Amateur, in which Ray was anxious to improve upon his advance to the third round the previous year. The New York area qualifying rounds were held at Winged Foot, a course that was familiar to Ray and which held the fond memory of his New York State championship of the previous year. He took advantage and broke the Winged Foot East course record with a 66 in the first round. Although he skied to an 80 in the second round, he qualified easily and was off to Garden City Golf Club on Long Island where he would eventually meet up with an opponent who became a central figure in his golf career.

Ray started off the tournament with a 4&2 win over Philip Simon and followed it with a 1-Up win in a tough match with New Jersey state champion Charles Whitehead. Three more wins followed: 3&2 over Carl Dann Jr., 3&2 over James McHale and 4&3 over Lawrence Lloyd. Ray was in the quarterfinals in just his second appearance in the National Amateur. Waiting there as his next opponent was none other than Johnny Goodman, the man who pulled off the big upset of Bob Jones in the first round of the 1929 Amateur at Pebble Beach, and who, in 1933, became the last amateur to win the U.S. Open. Winning the U.S. Amateur was more than Johnny's objective; it was his quest.

As would be the case several times in the future, Ray's match with Goodman came down to the last few holes. The first nine holes ended all-square after Ray came back from two down after the first three holes. He birdied the 5th and 8th holes to draw even. Goodman went one up on the 10th hole with a par, but Ray evened the match again at the 14th when Goodman bogeyed. After Ray visited two bunkers and took four shots to reach the green, he conceded the 15th. A bogey by Ray on the 16th and a halved 17th ended the match with a 2&1 Goodman victory. Johnny did not go on to win his first Amateur. He lost to eventual champion Johnny Fischer in the semifinals and would have to wait another year to continue his quest.

After the long season and with busyness in his sales job, Ray intended to end his golf year after the U.S. Amateur. He said "I had really planned to quit until spring." However, a special invitation changed his plans; he was selected to be a part of the Metropolitan New York team in the Lesley Cup matches. This event, which originated in 1905, featured individual and team play in inter-city competition among teams from Boston, New York and Philadelphia. It also includes a discussion of issues regarding the game of golf, which was still in its infancy in America at the time. Founder Robert W. Lesley believed that the yearly gathering would foster lofty standards for competition, sportsmanship, fellowship, and stewardship of the game. By the 1920s, the city teams had evolved into statewide teams from Massachusetts, Metropolitan New York and Pennsylvania. Quebec, Canada was included later in the decade. It is believed that the Lesley Cup became the model for the Walker Cup and Ryder Cup.

The 1936 matches were held at the Rockaway Hunt Club on Long Island. Ray's New York teammates included Tommy Tailer, George Dunlap and George Voigt, all of whom where opponents of his in regional and national tournaments. Ray won all three of his singles matches and all but one of his foursomes matches. The Metropolitan New York team won the event by a wide margin.

1936 Accomplishments

- Low Amateur in Metropolitan Open
- Set a new Course Record at Winged Foot East
- Reached the Finals of Metropolitan Amateur
- Reached the Finals of New York State Amateur
- Won the Sweetser Victory Cup
- Reached the Quarterfinals of U.S. Amateur
- Selected for New York Lesley Cup Team

1936 Metropolitan Amateur Caricature

5   Getting to the Finals

Although the Sweetser Victory Cup was his only championship outside of Dutchess County, Ray had accomplished much in 1936. He reached the finals of both the Metropolitan and New York State Amateurs and improved his finish in the U.S. Amateur by reaching the quarterfinals. His losses in the three tournaments were by the narrow margins of 1-Up, 1-Up and 2&1, respectively. He also improved his national standing. Famous sportswriter Bob Considine noted Ray's performances and commented that the Cinderella Kid was reaching the upper tier of amateur golf.

Ray spent the winter focused on his increasing responsibilities as a print salesman for Western Printing. He also continued his play in the company bowling league. Interestingly, he had captured the attention of the Poughkeepsie press to such an extent that his bowling scores received regular newspaper coverage. Ray did not forget about golf during the winter months. He added twenty pounds to his slender frame with the hope of strengthening his game.

The 1937 golf season did not start well. Ray had only one round under 75 in the Metropolitan Open at the Forest Hill Field Club in Bloomfield, New Jersey. His 299 total was seven shots behind low amateur Frank Strafaci, a former U.S. Public Links champion and one of the leading amateurs in the New York area. He finished twenty strokes behind the tournament winner, professional Jimmy Hines. A notable sidelight of the tournament was the appearance of 24-year-old Sam Snead, who was billed as "the sensation of the winter circuit."

Things did not get better for Ray in the Metropolitan Amateur at the Metropolis Country Club in White Plains, New York. He lost in the second round to relatively unknown John Parker in a 19-hole match. Poor putting hampered Ray's performance in the two Met tournaments. It would not be the last time that inconsistency on the greens hurt his tournament chances.

Things got better at the HRGA tournament in June. Ray was the low qualifier with a score of 70 at the Hudson River Country

Club in Yonkers, New York, and advanced to the match play finals where he routed Foster Nicholls of the home club, 11&10.

Success continued at the Sweetser Victory Cup, played over the Winged Foot East and West courses. Ray won the tournament for the second consecutive year and did so in spectacular fashion. His 283 total for the four rounds was five under par. It set a new tournament record by a whopping eleven strokes. The previous record holder was none other than Bob Jones. After a slow start to the year, the Cinderella Kid, now 23 years old, was suddenly playing the best golf of his life.

Next up was the New York State Amateur at the Oak Hill Country Club in Rochester. Oak Hill is one of the great American golf clubs. It features two courses designed by the legendary golden age architect Donald Ross, and it has hosted many of the major professional and amateur championships of the country, including three Opens, two Senior Opens, three PGAs, two Amateurs and a Ryder Cup.

Ray served notice that his game was in top form by tying the Oak Hill course record with a 66 in a practice round. But, demonstrating once again that golf is a very fickle game, he struggled to a 7-over-par 43 on the first nine holes of the medal play qualifying round that was played in a pouring rain. Fortunately, he steadied himself with an even-par 36 on the back nine for a score of 79 that barely got him into the 32-player match play field. By an unusual twist of fate in the pairings, his first-round opponent was Wes VanBenschoten, a Colgate University star and a fellow Dutchess club member. Ray won the "club members match" 2&1 and followed it with wins over Dudley Ward, 1-Up, and Bus Drexilius, 5&3, to reach the semifinals, where his opponent was Bill Holt Jr. whose score of 70 had won the qualifying medal. Ray prevailed, 1-Up.

The 36-hole final match was a repeat of the previous year's final: Ray versus Tommy Goodwin, a Winged Foot member and one of the leading amateurs in the New York metropolitan area. Goodwin won the 1936 title over Ray by a narrow 1-Up margin. This time it was different, very different. Ray was 5-Up after 18 holes, was 2-under-par after 27 holes, and went on to rout

Goodwin 11&9. The New York State title was his for the second time in three years, and he had won it convincingly.

Back in Poughkeepsie after the state tournament, Ray won the second of four straight Dutchess club championships by a hefty 11&10 margin over Frank Shanley, who happened to be the Club Captain. By now the Dutchess club members, as well as the citizens of Poughkeepsie, were "gaga" over Ray Billows and his state championships. The club and city had a true sports hero, and Ray's humble manner added to the plaudits he was given. So excited were the Dutchess members that they decided to hold an elaborate "Billows Day" at the club, including an exhibition golf match that they asked Ray to arrange. Ray was pleased to oblige and arranged for a match that featured himself and Tommy Goodwin versus Frank Strafaci and Bill Holt. That these highly regarded amateurs were willing to travel to an event that honored one of their competitors reflected the respect Ray had gained among his peers.

Billows Day took place in early August and it was a gala affair attended by more than 150 club members and guests. The local police were engaged to control traffic on the state highway alongside the club. A large tent with elaborate lighting was the scene of a barbecue dinner and evening dancing. Tommy Goodwin's birdie on the 17th hole clinched the exhibition match for him and Ray over Strafaci and Holt. The match featured several birdies and recovery shots that wowed the large crowd.

Ray decided to rest and practice before heading to the west coast for the U.S. Amateur. He turned down an invitation to play in the prestigious Anderson Memorial tournament at Winged Foot, as well as invitations to other area tournaments and exhibitions. He planned to travel by train with a stop and layover in Racine to visit relatives and old friends and play in an exhibition with his high school teammate Wilford Wehrle at the Racine Country Club, where they had met as caddies. Wehrle was the current Wisconsin State Amateur champion and a fellow qualifier for the national Amateur. They didn't know it at the time but Ray and Wehrle, who traveled together to the Amateur, were to meet again in the west.

The 1937 U.S. Amateur was played at the Alderwood Country Club in Portland, Oregon. The Alderwood golf course was designed by A. Vernon Macon, a native of Ireland who immigrated to British Columbia and became the busiest course designer in the Pacific Northwest. He was noted for bold designs and Alderwood was one of them. Located on the banks of the Columbia River and with Mt. Hood as a backdrop, it featured an unusual configuration of five Par 5s, five Par 3s and eight Par 4s. It was also considered a stern test.

Ray attracted the attention of both players and the press with a 4-under-par 68 in a practice round. Ted Husing, a star sports announcer for CBS, featured Ray in one of his pre-tournament broadcasts and labeled him the tournament darkhorse. He also noted that Ray's play had impressed the early gallery.

Starting with this edition of the Amateur, the USGA changed from what had been an all match play format to a 36-hole medal play qualifying round followed by match play among the low 64 qualifiers. Ray advanced to match play easily with a score of even-par 144, which tied for second in the competition for the qualifying medal. When the match play pairings were announced, Ray found himself in the first half of the draw with several outstanding players, among whom were medalist Roger Kelly, Chick Evans, Charles Kocsis, Frank Strafaci and defending champion Johnny Fischer.

After defeating Stanford student Robert Thompson easily by an 8&7 margin, Ray won 2&1 over Roy Wiggins, who had upset Tommy Goodwin in a 19-hole match. He then defeated the Michigan state champion and Walker Cup player Charles Kocsis, 3&2, to advance to the quarterfinals, where he won 2-Up over Reynolds Smith to reach the semifinals against defending champion Johnny Fischer. Johnny defeated "the grand old man of golf" Chick Evans 1-Up in the quarterfinals. In 1916 Evans became the first amateur to win the U.S. Amateur and U.S. Open in the same year.

Fischer had not been playing his best golf and things didn't improve enough in his 36-hole match with Ray. Johnny managed to stay close early and was only 1-Down after the morning 18 holes. But in the afternoon, it was not long before Ray's triumph was assured. He won the first three holes with two birdies and a par, drew 5-Up at the turn with a one-under-par 36, and ended the contest 6&5 on the 31st hole.

Ray Billows, the Cinderella Kid who some were now calling the "Cinderella Man," was in the finals of the U.S. Amateur! His opponent was Johnny Goodman, who defeated Marvin "Bud" Ward in his semifinal and was continuing his 8-year quest for the Amateur title. Johnny bested Ray in a close quarterfinal match in 1936 before losing to eventual champion Johnny Fischer. The man from humble beginnings in Nebraska was the favorite this year, but there was something about the young man from humble beginnings in Wisconsin that raised doubt.

Excitement was high for the final match. The record crowds of 5,000 that followed the earlier matches grew to 9,000 for the final. The match was aired on national radio by CBS, much to the delight of the players' enthusiastic fans in Omaha and Poughkeepsie. The stage was set for one of the best played and thrilling matches ever in a U.S. Amateur final.

Goodman got off to a fast 2-Up start when Ray bogeyed the difficult second hole and Johnny birdied the par-five 5th. Ray's birdie on the 8th reduced his deficit to one after the first nine. Another bogey by Ray on the 10th restored Goodman's lead to 2-Up but Ray's birdies on the next two holes evened the match. The see-sawing continued with a Billows bogey on the 13th and one by Goodman on the 14th. Two halved holes after a birdie by Goodman on the par-five 15th and a bogey by Ray on the par-three 16th ended the morning round with Goodman 2-Up. Johnny's medal score for the round was an even-par 72; Ray was only one shot higher at 73. The fun was just beginning.

Crack! That could have been the sound made when the face of Ray's brassie hit the ball on his second shot on the 501-yard par-five first hole of the afternoon round. The ball soared toward the green and ended up within eight inches of the cup. The conceded putt for an eagle three reduced Ray's deficit to one hole and sent a charge of excitement through the gallery. The excitement was dampened when Ray bogeyed the next hole to restore Goodman's

2-Up advantage. Ray reduced his deficit again on the 23rd hole but when Goodman birdied the 24th and Ray bogeyed the 25th and 28th Johnny's margin ballooned to 4-Up. Had the clock struck midnight for the Cinderella Kid? Four down with eight to play was a very deep hole to climb out of.

But wait. Wasn't this exactly the same deficit Ray faced in the final of the 1935 New York State Amateur when he startled the gallery with his comeback and then sat atop his flivver with the championship trophy? A comparison of the situations had to occur to him and be a source of encouragement, and Goodman's double bogey on the 29th hole had to strengthen his resolve. After the next three holes were halved, with both players alternating recoveries with missed birdie opportunities, Ray birdied the par-five 33rd to cut the lead to 2-Up. When Goodman missed the green on the par-three 34th and bogeyed the hole, it was just one down with two to play for Ray.

The gallery in Portland was abuzz and anxious ears were pressed against radios in Poughkeepsie. There was little doubt that most of the folks in both cities were pulling for the underdog Cinderella Kid.

Ray didn't have a chance to win the 35th after he pulled his tee shot nearly under a tree off the left side of the fairway. He sent a wonderful shot under the branches of the tree to the green, but the ball ended up 40 feet from the hole. Goodman reached the green in regulation, 60 feet away. When both players two-putted, the hole was halved and Johnny was dormie.

Ray's last chance was at the 561-yard par-five 36th hole; he needed to win the hole to square the match and force a playoff. He hit a remarkable 300-yard drive to the fairway; Goodman's tee shot was 70 yards behind Ray's, also in the fairway. After Johnny laid up safely to within pitching distance of the green, it was all-or-nothing time for Ray. He gave his second shot all he had in an effort to reach the green in two, but the ball faded to the right into a pear orchard on a downhill, grassy lie with pears all around. Goodman pitched to the green, seven feet from the hole. Ray, careful to avoid the pears near his ball, pitched onto the green but the ball ran 25 feet past the hole. When his putt rolled by the cup he extended his hand to concede Johnny's birdie putt and the match.

Johnny Goodman had fulfilled his long quest for the U.S. Amateur title. Underdog Ray Billows had made another stirring comeback that thrilled the gallery and elevated his status on the national stage. But the narrow loss in a winnable match was a disappointment for Ray. It wouldn't be his last such experience.

Sportsmanship abounded at the conclusion of the match. Ray's comment after the match was that he had tried his hardest "but a better golfer beat me." Movie footage of Ray's concession on the final green shows that he was smiling as he shook Goodman's hand. That gesture also wouldn't be his last such experience; he would become known for his gentlemanly character and graciousness. On Johnny's part, his post-match comment was: "I'm sorry Ray, that there aren't two titles awarded." The close match had convinced the nation's top amateur that he had a worthy challenger.

Ray did not return to Poughkeepsie immediately after the Amateur. Shortly after he arrived in Portland he announced that he was going to play in the Western Amateur in Los Angeles. This tournament, which is conducted by the Western Golf Association, was and remains one of the top amateur events in the country. In 1937 it was held at the Los Angeles Country Club on the club's North Course, which was designed by golden age architect George C. Thomas and is considered one of the classic American courses. The Walker Cup matches will be played there in 2017.

Ray got off to a shaky start with a six-over-par 42 on the front nine of the qualifying round but recovered with a two-under-par 33 on the back nine to qualify for match play. He continued his under-par play in winning his first three matches and defeated fellow New Yorker Bill Holt, 2&1, in the quarterfinals. Given his stellar play and his performance the previous week in Portland, Ray was considered the tournament favorite when he reached the semifinals against none other than Wilford Wehrle, the Wisconsin schoolmate with whom he had traveled west from Racine.

It was not to be for Ray. After 31 holes of back and forth play during which he came back three times from deficits to square the match, Ray overshot the green on the 32nd hole and hooked his tee shot on the 33rd. Two bogeys were the result and when the next two holes were halved, Wehrle had a 2&1 victory. Ray stayed around to watch his friend win the final match over Chuck Kocsis. The two then traveled back to Racine by train; from there Ray returned to Poughkeepsie, where a celebration was waiting to happen.

The folks in Poughkeepsie were, of course, very disappointed with Ray's two close losses in the U.S. and Western Amateurs. But they were also very proud of their fellow townsman. Plans were being made to welcome Ray home even before the final match in Portland got underway. As reported in a local newspaper: "He is to be met at the train, put in the back of an open-air car, and paraded uptown to the Nelson House hotel where he will receive the city's felicitations publicly from Mayor Spratt. After that there will be a citywide testimonial dinner in his honor. It is intended to have a band at the station to add to the rousing reception." The plans were modified later to include a dance at Dutchess Golf and Country Club after the dinner.

Despite a rainy September day, more than 300 people greeted Ray at the train station and 225 attended the sold-out dinner. Praise was heaped upon him by several of the city's luminaries. Mayor Spratt noted that he had raised Poughkeepsie's prestige across the nation and was providing the city "free publicity." The president of the Chamber of Commerce formally accorded him a niche in the Chamber's Corridor of Fame alongside such local traditions as Vassar College, Smith Brothers' Cough Drops, and the Intercollegiate Regatta.

Dutchess club president Walter Kingston praised Ray's humble nature and his willingness to play with club members regardless of their ability. He also presented Ray with an Honorary Lifetime Membership in the club with the comment: "The privilege is ours rather than his in knowing this man." There was even a message of commendation sent from President Roosevelt, whose family home is in nearby Hyde Park.

And so it went. Ray accepted it all in his usual unassuming manner. "This wouldn't be complete unless I get up and say Boy!

Getting to the Finals

Am I glad to be home again," said the young golfer. "I think this is one swell party." He declined to go further with a speech but agreed to answer questions, the biggest of which was "What happened on the final hole in Portland?"

More than one account of Ray's second shot on the hole had surfaced in the press. One said his ball rested on a submerged tree root that caused the clubface to open when his club hit it. Another claimed that a camera click affected his swing. Yet another said that he "pressed" in trying to reach the green in two. Ray seemed to agree, at least partially, with the last of these. His reply to the question was: "I made the mistake of figuring out my shot after I started to swing. I eased up and didn't get through the shot. It wasn't a matter of pressing, but – well, maybe it was – I don't know." Many years later in an interview, Ray attributed the result of the shot to the hidden tree root. The difference in his explanations is likely because he didn't want to appear to be making excuses at the dinner.

With the big celebration behind him, Ray closed out the golf season with a few local and area events. The most notable of these was the International Open in Belmont, Massachusetts. He won the award for the best performance by an amateur.

There was one more highlight in Ray's year, an anecdote that is a colorful part of his career. During his match with Johnny Goodman in the U.S. Amateur final, on the sixth hole Ray was stymied behind a large tree with no apparent shot to the green. He hit a low hook under and around the tree to within a few feet of the hole. Bob Jones, who was in the gallery with his friend Charlie Yates, remarked out loud: "I don't think anybody in the world could hit that shot better than Ray Billows." A man nearby, not recognizing Jones, disagreed, with the comment: "Bobby Jones could hit that shot with his eyes closed." Jones, not revealing his identity, said: "I'm not so sure he could." "Mister," the man replied somewhat angrily, "have you ever seen that son-of-a-bitch play?" Jones looked at the man and said: "Can't say that I have."

As the year ended Ray reaffirmed his intention to remain an amateur. "Professional golfers are not making any money," he said. "I figure that the contacts I am making as an amateur will be worth more to me in a business and monetary way than I could possibly make as a professional. I'm staying amateur."

1937 Accomplishments

- Won HRGA Championship
- Won Sweetser Victory Cup
- Won New York State Amateur
- Reached the Semifinals of Western Amateur
- Reached the Finals of U.S. Amateur
- Ranked the #2 Amateur in the U.S.

1937 U.S. Amateur Poster

6   The Walker Cup and a Duke

In an October, 1937 interview, Walker Cup Captain Francis Ouimet was asked to compare the top amateurs of the day with those of the early Walker Cup players of the 1920s. Conceding that he might be prejudiced in favor of the veterans, and mentioning names of the past such as Bob Jones, George Von Elm, Jess Sweetser, Bob Gardner and himself, he named only three current players who he thought could "stand up to" the veterans: Johnny Goodman, Johnny Fischer and Lawson Little. Obviously, and despite his accomplishments during the year, Ray Billows was not one of the names.

Nonetheless, when the USGA committee responsible for selecting the U.S. team for the 1938 Walker Cup match met in January, Ray was one of the selections, as were Johnny Goodman and Johnny Fischer; Lawson Little was not. Also not selected were Wilford Wehrle and Frank Strafaci, omissions that caused a bit of a stir in the national press.

Ray and the Poughkeepsie community were thrilled. Being a member of a Walker Cup team was and remains one of the highest honors an amateur golfer can attain. Ray would be referred to as a "Walker Cupper" often over the years, especially in the local press. When asked in later years about his best experience in golf, the Walker Cup was always Ray's response.

The 1938 Walker Cup was played in early June at the "Home of Golf," St. Andrews in Scotland. It was preceded by the British Amateur at the Royal Troon Golf Club, a tournament in which the American team players were invited to play. The combination of two tournaments and transatlantic travel by ship made the trip to Scotland a lengthy one. The team would leave on May 10 and not arrive back in the U.S. until June 14.

The timing and length of the trip complicated things for Ray. Given the northeastern winter, he was concerned about having sufficient preparation time and about the effect of the long trip on his readiness for the Metropolitan Amateur and HRGA tournaments, which were scheduled for the second half of June. He continued bowling in the company league as one way to keep in physical shape. Favorable late winter weather made it possible for him to practice at the Dutchess course. The course wasn't yet open to members but the club allowed him to use it. He got in some rounds at Winged Foot as well. Its location 60 miles to the south usually allowed it to open earlier than the Poughkeepsie courses.

Two other winter happenings are noteworthy. Ray accepted a position as the head of one of the major divisions of the Poughkeepsie Community Chest Drive. It was one of several civic contributions he would make over the years. In an opposite direction, he declined an invitation from Bob Jones to play in the Masters Tournament, as well as several other invitations from southern tournaments. Regretfully, he couldn't afford more time away from his job in addition to the month-long Walker Cup absence. There would be other Masters opportunities.

On the eve of his departure for Scotland, Ray was given a farewell dinner hosted by Poughkeepsie mayor Spratt. It was another in what would become a continuing stream of dinners in honor of the city's golf hero. Ray had little choice but to get comfortable on the "rubber chicken" dinner circuit.

At midnight on May 10, the United States Walker Cup team sailed for Great Britain on the S.S. Bremen. After arriving in Southampton, England they traveled to London, where they stayed for two days before going to Scotland. While in London the team was treated to a dinner at the U.S. Embassy. The dinner was hosted by Ambassador Joseph Kennedy, the father of future U.S. president JFK. The event became the scene of a colorful Ray Billows anecdote.

A guest at the dinner was England's Duke of Windsor, the former King Edward VIII, who abdicated the throne to marry American divorcee Wallis Simpson. Ray happened to be seated at the same table as the duke. Ray was probably unfamiliar with the formality of British royalty, but he had a playful sense of humor. "Hey Duke," he said, and continued with "do you play golf?" The duke ignored the informal salutation; he said that he did play but was having a tough time with a slice and with understanding how to grip a golf club properly. Ray picked up a dinner knife and proceeded to conduct a grip lesson for the former king. The duke was both impressed and pleased. He presented Ray his necktie as a gift. Unfortunately, this unique and valuable artifact is lost. Ray's daughter Barbara remembers a blue tie being draped around a lampshade in her father's house (Ray was informal as well as playful) but its location today is a mystery.

When British Amateur play started at Troon, Ray was one of the participants. During the winter when he was concerned about his preparation, he had said he would play only if he felt his game was ready. Apparently, he felt it was. As things turned out, it was not. He managed to win his first match against Raymond Quilter of England. His opponent in the second round was Johnny Goodman. That the two highest-ranking American amateurs ended up playing against each other in such an early round of the tournament was a curious pairings twist.

Over the years, one of the notable things about Ray's career was that he almost always avenged defeats by beating players he had lost to previously. The exception was Johnny Goodman. Although their matches were very closely played, there is no record of Ray ever defeating Johnny in match play. Such was the case at Troon. Goodman won, 3&2, in a match where neither Johnny nor Ray played very well.

The 1938 British Amateur was won by American Charlie Yates, a colorful and light-hearted player from Atlanta who delighted the British crowds and press with his antics. He defeated Cecil Ewing in the final match. Ray would meet up with both Yates and Ewing at the Walker Cup Match; Charlie would become one of his lifetime friends. All three of them were off to St. Andrews.

The Walker Cup Match (not "Matches") started unofficially in 1921 when a group of American amateurs traveled to Royal Liverpool Golf Club (Hoylake) in England to participate in the British Amateur tournament. Chairman of the club Gershom Stewart proposed the informal match with British amateurs, and it was held prior to the start of the Amateur. The match started officially in 1922, was held annually through 1925 and then biannually since 1926. It is named after George Herbert Walker, who was the USGA president when the official match began. He is the namesake and grandfather of George H.W. Bush and the great grandfather of George W. Bush, the 41st and 43rd presidents of the United States.

The format in the 1938 match was four foursomes (alternate shot) matches on the first day followed by eight singles matches on the second day, with all matches played over 36 holes. American teams had won the previous nine matches, often by wide margins. The Americans were heavily favored to win again, so much so that most U.S. newspapers trumpeted that there was no way the team could lose. As a Chicago newspaper did in 1948 when it declared Thomas Dewey a presidential winner over Harry Truman, the newspapers got it wrong. The team from Great Britain and Ireland won its first Walker Cup fairly easily, 7½ to 4½.

Ray was paired with Charlie Yates in a foursomes match against Englishman Charlie Stowe and Scot Alex Kyle. Ray and Charlie won, 3&2; it was the only American win in foursomes play. In singles play Ray faced Cecil Ewing from Ireland, a large man noted for his booming tee shots. Ewing played in six Walker Cups and served as captain and president of the Golfing Union of Ireland. Surprisingly, he did not play in the foursomes matches.

The singles match was closely played. Ewing got off to a solid start by winning the first two holes of the morning round, the first with a birdie and the second when Ray had a double bogey. The match became all-square when Ewing made double bogey on the 3rd and Ray birdied the par-five 5th. A birdie on the 9th gave Ray a 1-Up lead at the turn, a lead he maintained to the end of the morning when each player won a hole on the back nine and seven holes were halved.

Ewing squared the match on the first hole of the afternoon round with a birdie and built a 2-Up lead at the turn with birdies on the 5th and 6th holes. Ray squared the match again when he won the 15th and 16th holes, but Ewing's par on the difficult 17th (the famous Road Hole) gave him a 1-Up lead, and the match when both players made par on the 18th. Ray's very good afternoon medal score of 72 in difficult weather wasn't good enough against the Irishman's two-under-par 70.

Ray's first Walker Cup experience ended with a win and a loss. He was satisfied with that, especially given the nature of his match with Cecil Ewing, but he was disappointed with the team's loss. The long journey to Scotland ended when the S.S. Berengaria sailed into New York City harbor on June 14. There was little time to rest. Match play in the Metropolitan Amateur began two days later at Ridgewood Country Club in New Jersey. Some relief was provided when Walker Cup players were allowed to enter without needing to qualify.

Apparently, Ray did not have a hangover from the Walker Cup trip. He won his first match in the Met Amateur over Alpheus Winter Jr. by a comfortable 6&5 margin and went on to win again against John Burke, 3&2. His run ended when he lost, 3&2, to Frank Strafaci in the semifinals. Frank went on to win the tournament, perhaps motivated by his exclusion from the Walker Cup team. He defeated Willie Turnesa, another Walker Cup team member, in the final.

No rest for the weary. The HRGA Championship took place on the following weekend at Ray's home Dutchess course. He won the qualifying medal with a score of 71 and went on to win his third championship in four years by easily defeating fellow Dutchess member Wes VanBenschoten, 7&6, in the final match.
Next came the Sweetser Victory Cup at Winged Foot in early July. Ray won the medal play tournament for the third consecutive year, this time by eight shots over Dick Chapman of the home club. In the second round he narrowly missed tying the Winged Foot West course record of 68 when he missed a two-foot putt on the 18th green.

Then it was on to the New York State Amateur at the Quaker Ridge Golf Club in Scarsdale. Ray qualified with a score of 71, one stroke behind medalist Tommy Goodwin. In match play he was 3-Up after four holes in defeating William Stark, 4&2; he won over Raymond Korndorfer 2&1, and bested Martin Speno 6&4 to reach the semifinals. There he lost to old foe and friend Willie Turnesa on the 22nd hole when Willie sank a 25-foot birdie putt.

Ray's last major tournament of the year was the U.S. Amateur, which was played at the famous and very difficult Oakmont

Country Club course outside of Pittsburgh, Pennsylvania. The tournament was beset by rain that never seemed to stop and which made the course even more difficult than usual. Whether it was the rainy conditions or the state of his game, Ray did not play well. His mediocre 153 qualifying score got him to match play, where he defeated Johnny Levinson, a former New England champion, in a seesaw 20-hole match. Ray looked to have the match won on the 18th hole when Levinson hooked into the rough off the tee. But the Maine native hit a marvelous 2-iron shot to four feet and sank the birdie putt to force extra holes. After the 19th hole was halved, Levinson hooked another drive into the rough on the 20th hole, but this time he could not recover.

Pat Abbott, a part-time actor from California and a former U.S. Public Links champion, eliminated Ray in the second round, 3&1, in a match where Ray never led. Abbott advanced to the final match where he lost to Willie Turnesa.

Ray was not the only victim at rain-soaked Oakmont. British Amateur winner Charlie Yates, Bud Ward, Fred Haas, highly ranked Canadian Ross Somerville, and the previous year's medalist Roger Kelly all lost in early rounds. Nonetheless, Ray's performance was a significant disappointment for him.

Speaking of Ross Somerville, in an interview Ray stated that he thought Ross was "the best amateur golfer in the world today." It was a surprising statement given all the top-flight amateurs Ray knew and had played against. His explanation was simple: "He's all golf. He concentrates on every shot harder than any man I've ever seen."

The interview also revealed an interesting contrast between Ray's approach to match play compared with that of Bob Jones, a man considered the best amateur of all time. Jones advocated an approach of forgetting about your opponent and concentrating on "Old Man Par." He said if you made par on every hole you would win the match. Ray disagreed. He said: "I always watch my opponent and try to match him stroke for stroke. That's the way to beat him. If he drives 250 yards, I try to drive 275. If you can do a little better than your opponent on every stroke, you're bound to win." In contrast, Ray's approach to medal play was "Play safe golf."

Ray was also asked to name his favorite club. His response was the niblick, which was the equivalent of today's 9-iron. Given Ray's reputation with the driver and irons, particularly the long irons, his choice of the niblick reflects a focus on the short game. The great Byron Nelson, with whom Ray played some exhibitions, claimed that Ray was the best long iron player in the game at the time, amateur or professional.

****

Some shock waves rippled through amateur golf in September of 1938. The tremors were especially intense in the Poughkeepsie community. A statement from Ray implied that he might be retiring from golf. The statement was so unexpected that it triggered rumors, including a seemingly incredulous one that Ray was retiring to spend more time with a new favorite sport of fishing. A fishing trip to Canada with Jimmy Peelor and his father may have sparked the rumor.

What Ray actually said was: "It is very doubtful that I will play in the National Amateur next year. I won't be playing much golf from now on due to the pressure of business affairs." It wasn't exactly a retirement announcement, but it was ominous. What had caused it? Was it really business pressure as his printing sales responsibilities grew? Was it frustration with his performance at Oakmont in the U.S. Amateur? Could it possibly have anything to do with fishing?

Whatever it was, it turned out not to be true. Ray Billows was going to have a big year in 1939, both in golf and personally.

1938 Accomplishments

- Selected for the Walker Cup Team (1-1 record)
- Reached the Semifinals of Metropolitan Amateur
- Won the HRGA Championship (third in four years)
- Won the Sweetser Victory Cup (third consecutive)

Putting at Winged Foot

7   The Masters, the U.S. Amateur, and a Strawberry Blonde

1939 got off to an awkward start for Ray. While in New York City on a business trip, he got a traffic ticket for driving too close to a trolley car at 42nd Street and Ninth Avenue. Whether he tried to talk the magistrate out of the fine is not known, but he paid $3 to what a Poughkeepsie newspaper called the "big city."

Things got better when Ray received another invitation to the Masters Tournament from Bob Jones. This time he accepted, but there was an odd twist. Ray claimed that he would play in the tournament as part of a business trip to Atlanta, which was the home of both Jones and his fellow amateur and friend Charlie Yates. It was reported that Jones would accompany him in one or two of his business meetings, which seems remarkable given Jones' status, but it reflected of Bob's support of amateur golfers. Amateurs have always been a part of the prestigious tournament originated by Bob Jones.

In commenting about the Masters invitation, Ray signaled that he was not "through with golf" as had been interpreted from his remarks at the end of 1938. He said that he planned to play in the Metropolitan and New York State Amateurs. But, he also said: "My season's golf will be according to my business plans. I cannot make plans way ahead." Ray made another comment that he did not expect to play well in the Masters because of his lack of practice. The two topics – business conflict and practice time – are important in evaluating Ray's ultimate ranking among his peers. Clearly, he did not play as much golf as most of them.

Ray's prediction about his Masters play was accurate. His score of 313 left him 41st in the field. But he left Augusta with something special – a $1.00 check with Bob Jones' signature on it. Jones had a standard $1 wager in a match with any amateur who played with him in a Masters practice round. Ray won his match and asked Jones if he would pay him with a check. Bob's response was: "Of course, I do it all the time because nobody ever cashes the check." The check was one of Ray's most cherished possessions. It now has s with one of his grandchildren.

...y returned home from Augusta he sent Bob Jones a ...nked him for the Masters invitation and related how ...oyed the experience. Bob responded with a letter in which ... ...nked Ray for the "nice note" and went on to say: "I shall certainly see you at the Amateur, if not before, and hope very much that we may have a game soon." Was Bob looking for a return match to win his dollar back? Most likely not; it was another example of his courtesy to amateurs.

Another pair of letters signaled some tension in Ray's job environment. In April he sent a handwritten interoffice communication to H.M. Benstead, the site manager of Western Printing's Poughkeepsie facility. Its stated purpose was "to drop you a line regarding my golf this year." In it Ray mentioned that the number of tournaments he would play in would be governed by the amount of work he had at the office, and that he planned to play in the Metropolitan, New York State and National Amateurs. It appears that the primary purpose of the note was to get the manager's reaction to adding the U.S. Open to his schedule. The communication ended with: "Will you please let me have your opinion regarding this."

Benstead's response was a typewritten letter in which he said he was referring the matter to company president Wadewitz. However, he went on for a page and a half to state "my own feelings." In a nutshell, those feelings were that Ray should spend more time servicing customers and learning about the printing business than playing golf, and that his golf should be restricted to his vacation time (although he also said that he was very much in favor of Ray's golf with prospective customers during working days). There's no documented record of the aftermath of the situation, but it is easy to predict president Wadewitz's reaction. It was because of golf that he gave Ray a job with his company, and his feelings about Ray's tournament play were demonstrated when he flew from Racine to New York on the spur of the moment to see Ray's final match in the 1935 New York State Amateur. Ray's golf schedule was not affected significantly at the time, but the work-versus-golf issue did have some impact in future years.

Ray did try to qualify for the U.S. Open but failed to do so. His major tournament season started with the Metropolitan Amateur, which was played in mid-June at the Nassau Country Club on Long Island. Ray won three matches to advance to the semifinals where he lost to Dick Chapman in a 20-hole match. Hooked drives in regulation play and on the 20th hole cost him an opportunity for his first win in the event. The tournament was won for the second consecutive year by Frank Strafaci.

In late June, Ray was the medalist in the HRGA tournament but lost in the second round of match play to youngster Grant Birkenhead, a fellow Dutchess club member. Ray made a generous gesture at the event. He returned for future use the tournament trophy that he retired with his third win in the previous year. Next came the Sweetser Victory Cup, which Ray had won in each of the three previous years. He finished tied for second and lost to Charley Pettijohn in a 3-hole playoff to finish third.

At an invitational tournament in Rye, New York in late July Ray came in contact with baseball great Babe Ruth. "The Babe" was impressed with Ray's drives but thought he could do better and challenged him to a contest for a dollar a drive. After 17 drives, Ray had $17 of Ruth's money and The Babe thought that was enough.

The New York State Amateur was played at Siwanoy Country Club, a Donald Ross course in Bronxville. Ray won three matches by comfortable margins to reach the semifinals against Dick Chapman, to whom he had lost on the 20th hole in the semifinals of the Metropolitan Amateur earlier in the year. In a match that featured excellent golf by both players, Ray lost again, 2-Up. Chapman's medal score was two-under-par 69; Ray was even-par.

At the Eastern Amateur in Syracuse, New York at the Syracuse Yacht and Country Club, Ray lost a second-round match to Paul Guenther, 2-Up. He also lost a putter in a less than usual way that created another colorful anecdote.

The putter story began at the New York State Amateur, to which Ray brought a new mallet-head putter in place of the usual blade style he had used for years. Art Morris, one of his friends, believed that the putter cost him a chance to advance further in the state tournament and threatened to do something about it with the comment: "If you come to the Eastern Amateur with that club I'll throw it in the lake." Ray didn't take his friend at his word and brought the mallet to Syracuse. Art proved himself as good as his word; when Ray putted poorly and was eliminated from the Eastern Amateur, he, with Ray's blessing, heaved the putter far into the lake. When Ray talked about being reimbursed for the cost of the putter, Morris answered that he was doing him a favor and that Ray should be paying him.

1939's last major tournament was the U.S. Amateur, which was held at the North Shore Golf Club in Glenview, Illinois outside of Chicago. Six years earlier the North Shore club hosted the last U.S. Open won by an amateur. That man was Johnny Goodman, and he was at the course again for the Amateur. Moreover, he was in the same half of the match play pairings as Ray, the man he had beaten on the 36th hole of the 1937 Amateur final. Would the two meet again?

Ray decided to break up the trip to Chicago by stopping in Racine for some business matters and to visit family and friends in the area. One of those friends was his old high school teammate Wilford Wehrle, who had also qualified for the Amateur. The two decided to enter the Meadowbrook Invitational 4-Ball Tournament in Detroit, as did some of Ray's amateur foes from the east with amateurs from the Detroit area as their partners. Ray and Wehrle defeated Willie Turnesa and Harvey Fruehauf, 2&1, in the semifinals, and won the event by defeating Dick Chapman and Tom Sheehan in the final, 1-Up. It was then off to Chicago for the Amateur. Except that Wehrle didn't get to play. A well-respected amateur who had good finishes in U.S. Opens and had won the Western Amateur, Wilford never had much luck in the U.S. Amateur. His bad luck this time was an emergency appendectomy.

Ray was playing well when he reached North Shore and his good play continued. He defeated Pat Mucci, 4&3, and then Henry Kowal, 4&2. Kowal was a Colgate University star who eventually moved to Poughkeepsie as a hotel manager and joined the Dutchess club. He and Ray became both opponents and partners in future area and state tournaments. Ray's third-round opponent was John Burke, who had won the NCAA Individual

Championship in 1938 as a Georgetown University student. Ray won, 2&1, to reach the quarterfinals against a man who he had once called the best amateur in the game, Ross Somerville. He might have changed his mind after he defeated the Canadian easily, 6&5.

In the semifinals Ray met the man who prevented a potential "revenge match" with Johnny Goodman. Texan Don Schumacher defeated Goodman in the second round, 1-Up, and won two more matches to reach the semifinal with Ray. It was no contest. Ray won the first six holes, built his lead to eight holes by the end of the morning round, and coasted to a 6&5 win to reach the Amateur final for the second time.

Meanwhile, on the other side of the draw, Marvin "Bud" Ward was continuing his sizzling summer play, which included turning in the lowest score ever by an amateur in the U.S. Open and missing a playoff for the championship by one stroke in a tournament won by the great Byron Nelson. In a tough match against Art Doering in the Amateur semifinal that he won 2&1, Ward had a five-under-par 67 in one of the sessions.

There was no mystery about how Ray and Ward reached the final. Ray was nine under par for 92 holes of match play; Ward was twelve under for 103 holes. Plus, both players were putting remarkably well.

So, the stage was set for Ray, dubbed "a little fellow with a big heart" by a sportswriter, against Ward, who was considered the best amateur in the country and the clear favorite in the match. Everybody expected a classic tight match.

It didn't happen. After he lost two of the first three holes, Ray battled back to square the match on the 8th hole. But, when he 3-putted the 9th and had two more 3-putts on the back nine, Ward had a 4-Up lead at the halfway mark. A sportswriter commented that Ray's putter, which reportedly had been given to him by his friend Charlie Yates, "was a torturous instrument in his hands." Ray cut into Ward's lead a few times during the afternoon round, but each was followed by a spell of poor putting. When Ward won the 31st hole with a birdie, he won the match and the championship by a 7&5 margin.

As he had done two years earlier in his finals match with Johnny Goodman, Ray had battled hard against a favored opponent, and had captured the fancy and support of the galleries. But he now knew the frustration of missing a second opportunity to win the National Amateur.

Charlie Yates, who was known for his playfulness, provided an amusing sidelight to the final match. He loaned Ray a funky white linen cap (see photos insert) as a good luck charm. It was the same cap Charlie wore when he won the British Amateur title in 1938. Ray wore the cap throughout his match with Bud Ward, but its charm did not carry over from Charlie to him.

****

On September 15, while Ray was playing his semifinal match in the Amateur, the following headline appeared in the *Poughkeepsie Eagle-News*:

Elinor L. Jaminet Engaged to Marry Raymond E. Billows

Where did that come from? In a newspaper that had carried virtually everything about Ray Billows and many newsy items about his Dutchess club, there had not been anything to suggest a relationship, let alone an engagement. Who was this girl? How did they meet? How long had they known each other?

This girl was quite a young lady. She was from a prominent Poughkeepsie family, was educated at private elementary and high schools and was a graduate of Wellesley College, Class of 1937. She and her family were members of the Poughkeepsie Tennis Club, where she was the Women's Tennis Champion, and the Dutchess Golf and Country Club. She was a member of the Poughkeepsie branch of the American Association of University Women and a chapter of the Daughters of the American Revolution.

Elinor Jaminet was also a beautiful and charming young woman with strawberry blonde hair who was a target for many of the single young men at the Poughkeepsie Tennis Club. She and

Ray probably met sometime in 1938 or early 1939. As the story goes, their meeting was arranged by Winnie Peelor, wife of Ray's friend and fellow Dutchess golfer Jim Peelor. During a conversation at the club, Winnie asked Ray why he wasn't seen with young ladies. Ray said that in addition to the time demands of golf and work, he was "particular" about girls. His explanation was that he liked redheads. (His daughter Barbara says that his favorite actor was Maureen O'Hara.)

Eureka! Winnie Peelor immediately thought of her good friend Elinor and her strawberry blonde hair. With Ray's agreement, Winnie set up a lunch date at the club for the two to meet. The meeting was more than a bit awkward for Ray because of his shyness, but he was smitten with Elinor, who would later tell Winnie that her first impression of Ray was that he was "cute."

Although he was not confident about his chances with Elinor because of their very different upbringings, Ray began to ask her out on dates. It was not easy. Elinor had lots of dates, many with guys from the tennis club. Ray had some success but he came up with an uncommon and aggressive way of getting to see Elinor more often. He would wait near her house for her to return from dates and then strike up a conversation after her date drove away. He soon grew frustrated with the situation and confronted Elinor about her other dates and his desire to be her first choice. She confided that her other dates were mostly with guys that she grew up with and that they were just friends. Realizing that their feelings for each other were mutual, the young couple began to see each other frequently. It didn't take long for Ray to propose marriage. His redhead said "Yes!"

When their engagement was announced to Elinor's parents, it was not received warmly. Leon and Loretta Jaminet were concerned about the difference in the backgrounds of Ray and their daughter. Leon, who owned a very successful electrical supplies company, may have been concerned about Ray's prospects as a salesman who played a lot of golf. Loretta may have been concerned about a difference in social standing. But, most importantly, both parents were definitely concerned about a difference in religion.

47

The Jaminet family was Presbyterian. Ray was Catholic. In the 1930s, so-called mixed marriages were frowned upon by both religions, and often by the individuals who practiced them. There were potential practical problems as well, such as which church to attend, how to raise children, etc. In fact, the Catholic Church required of both parties in a mixed marriage a written promise to raise children in the Catholic faith.

Ray addressed the situation aggressively with Leon and Loretta. He told them that he did not require or expect Elinor to change her religion, and that he definitely was not going to change his because of his promise to his mother on her deathbed. He also told them, emphatically, that he and Elinor were going to get married one way or another, and that they were sure that they could work things out. The parents, reluctantly, relented.

Ray and Elinor were married by a Catholic monsignor in the Jaminet home on November 22, 1939. Elinor's sister Marjorie was the maid of honor; Jim Peelor was the best man. After a short wedding trip to New York City the couple moved into a house on Longview Avenue in Poughkeepsie.

The couple's relationship and love grew over the years and they did indeed "work things out." Ray's daughter Barbara recalls that her mother was very devoted to Ray. She was understanding with respect to the demands of both his golf and his job, and she supported him unconditionally. As for Ray, his fondness for Elinor never wavered. He called her, affectionately, "Toots" and "Blondie." Ray and Elinor, best friends as well as married couple, enjoyed their life together.

Barbara also recalls that she sometimes attended two church services on Sunday, one Presbyterian with her mother and one Catholic with her father.

1939 Accomplishments

- Reached the Semifinals of Metropolitan Amateur
- Reached the Semifinals of New York State Amateur
- Won Meadowbrook 4-Ball with Wilford Wehrle
- Reached the Finals of U.S. Amateur
- Married Elinor Jaminet

Bud Ward and Ray with the Havemeyer Trophy

1935 New York State Amateur – The Cinderella Kid

Early Years

With Johnny Goodman – 1936 U.S. Amateur Quarterfinals

1937 U.S. Amateur Final – Goodman-Billows

1937: "I don't think anybody in the world could hit that shot better than Ray Billows"   - Bob Jones

1938 Walker Cup Team

St. Andrews - Over the Swilcan Burn

1939 Masters – Winnings from Bob Jones

*1939 U.S. Amateur Final – Concession to Marvin "Bud" Ward
(Notice Ray's Linen Cap, on Loan from Charlie Yates)*

1940 Masters: Hole In One on #16 – In on the Fly

1940 U.S. Amateur Preview

Family: Ned, Barbara, Ray, Elinor

With his ever-present pipe

Hero of the Winged Foot Caddies – East Course Record

Exhibition with Byron Nelson

1948 U.S. Amateur Final – Willie Turnesa

1949 Walker Cup Team
Top Row: McCormick, Bishop, Ouimet, McHale, Coe, Dawson
Bottom Row: Stranahan, Kocsis, Billows, Turnesa, Riegel

FELLOW AMATEURS

Pat Abbott

Jess Sweetser

Johnny Fischer

Frank Strafaci

"Bud" Ward

Wilford Wehrle

Charlie Yates

Frank Stranahan

8   The Wrong Time to Get Sick

As 1940 got underway the newlyweds settled into their first winter together. Ray focused on his sales job and continued to bowl in the Western Printing league. In January he was asked by *Poughkeepsie Evening Star & Enterprise* sportswriter Ed Rozell to offer suggestions for improving golf participation in the area. He offered three ideas: exhibitions by professionals and top amateurs, a Hudson Valley amateur tournament, and reciprocal playing privileges among all HRGA clubs. In time, all three ideas were implemented. During the year, he handled the exhibitions suggestion personally.

The biggest news of the winter was yet another of the annual statements by Ray about his retirement plans. This time there seemed to be more certainty than ever – 1940 would be his last year to participate in major tournaments. He added that he planned to play in as many tournaments as he could during the year in order to get well prepared for a (perhaps final) try for the U.S. Amateur, which was to be played at the Winged Foot course that he knew so well and where he had much success. The Cinderella Kid was going back to where the nickname started.

As spring approached Ray got the news that he was one of only four players to be given a scratch handicap by the Metropolitan Golf Association. The others were Dick Chapman, Frank Strafaci and Willie Turnesa. Ray made some news of his own when he decided to accept an invitation to play in the Masters Tournament. As usual, he cited lack of practice and play during the winter as the reason he didn't expect to finish well in the event.

His prediction was accurate overall, but there was a highlight with "a cherry on top." In the third round he shot a one-under-par 71 that included four birdies and – drum roll – a hole in one! The "ace" was made with an 8-iron on the 16th hole, which was 145 yards long at the time. The ball went into the cup on the fly, which left black marks from the flagstick paint as a permanent reminder of the shot. It was the third Masters hole in one; the first was made by amateur Ross Somerville on the same hole in 1934. There have been 27 holes in one at the Masters, only five of which have been made by amateurs. In addition to Somerville and Ray, the other amateurs are Billy Joe Patton, John Dawson and Bill Hyndman.

After his return from Augusta, Ray practiced to get ready for the Metropolitan Open, which was played in late May at the Forest Hill Country Club in Bloomfield, New Jersey. He was more than ready. His 66 in the first round was the lowest score by an amateur in the 35-year history of the tournament. His 282 total for the four rounds won the medal for low amateur, and he finished fifth overall.

Ray was far less successful in his next two events. He failed to qualify for the U.S. Open with a 151 score at the Mt. Vernon Country Club in Tuckahoe, New York. At the Metropolitan Amateur at Century Country Club in Purchase, New York he qualified for match play with a mediocre 153 but lost in the second round to "unknown" Johnny Gerlin who was just out of high school.

Taking a break from tournament play, Ray followed up on his January suggestion for exhibition matches by arranging one with three of his amateur friends at his Dutchess club in June. He was joined by Frank Strafaci (his partner in the exhibition match), Tommy Goodwin and Willie Turnesa. Willie was making his first of what would be several appearances at Dutchess over the years. More than 500 spectators watched an exciting match end in a tie after a seesaw battle. Turnesa had the low individual score, a 71. Ray and Goodwin had 72s and Strafaci a 73.

Ray got back to tournament play at the HRGA tournament at the Orange County Country Club in Middletown, New York. He won both medalist honors and his fourth individual championship. He defeated fellow Dutchess member Noel DeCordova in the final match, 5&4.

Next it was on to the Robert Todd Lincoln Memorial Cup at the Ekwanok Country Club in Manchester, Vermont. The club was founded in 1899 with a course designed by "The Old Man" Walter Travis and John Duncan Dunn. Ekwanok is a historic golf club. The Vermont Golf Association was formed there in 1902 and the club became the site of the state's amateur championship tournament. In 1914 the club hosted the U.S. Amateur, which was won by Francis Ouimet in a finals match against Jerome Travers.

Robert Todd Lincoln, the first son of President Abraham Lincoln, became the third president of the club in 1904 and served until his death in 1926. In 1928 the Robert Todd Lincoln Memorial Cup event was started in his honor as an invitational tournament that grew to include leading amateurs from the Mid-Atlantic and New England areas. The Ekwanok tournament is perhaps the best example of the many regional amateur tournaments in which Ray played. It continues to this day as a popular member-guest tournament.

In 1940 Ray won his first of six Robert Todd Lincoln Cups by defeating Kenny Corcoran in the final, 3&1. His other titles were in 1946, 1948, 1950, 1951 and 1954.

Because of business pressures, Ray did not play in the 1940 Sweetser Victory Cup, a tournament that he had won three times in the previous four years. For the same reason, he did not participate in the Dutchess Club Championship. His next tournament competition was in the New York State Amateur at the Onondaga Golf and Country Club in Syracuse. The event featured another of Ray's memorable encounters with Willie Turnesa.

After qualifying for match play with a 71, second to Turnesa's 69, Ray advanced to meet Princeton student Arnold Zimmerman in a quarterfinal match that was expected to be an easy one for him. It wasn't; Ray was 3-Down after nine holes. He battled back and gained a 1-Up advantage on the 17th hole, only to lose it when Zimmerman holed a 20-foot putt to win the 18th. Ray won the match on the 19th hole with a birdie. In the meantime, Willie Turnesa was burning up the course with a 67 in his quarterfinal match, only to find himself 2-Down to Bill Holt after 15 holes. Remarkably, Willie birdied each of the last three holes to win the match. After both players won their semifinal match in less dramatic fashion, the stage was set for a Billows-Turnesa final that was expected to be both electric and close.

It was electric, but it wasn't close. Ray was 8-under-par for 30 holes and won easily, 8&6, for his third New York State title. Willie's post-match comments explained one of his worst defeats.

He said that Ray's power was too much for him. He noted that Ray had thickened out physically and lengthened the arc of his swing. "He's making his added weight count for distance and has picked up 20 yards or so off the tee," said Willie. "I used to stay abreast of him on my drives, but he forced me to play the odd consistently."

Ray continued with his preparation plan for the U.S. Amateur by entering the Eastern Amateur at the Briar Hills Golf Club in Briarcliff Manor, New York. The Eastern, known until two years previous as the Syracuse Invitational, had expanded rapidly and was drawing the leading amateurs from throughout the east. Ray had not always played in the tournament, but this was his last opportunity for competitive play before the National Amateur. He advanced to the final where he met a familiar opponent, Tommy Goodwin. Ray was 3-Down after the first nine of their 36-hole match. It took him until the 12th hole of the afternoon round to gain the lead; from there he went on to win, 2&1.

All that was left in the year for Ray was the National Amateur at Winged Foot, the elusive championship that he yearned for, the one for which he had prepared more vigorously than any other in his life.

The buildup for the tournament was tremendous in the New York metropolitan area and, of course, in Poughkeepsie. It seemed that every sportswriter had something to say. One of them said, in effect, that The Cinderella Kid was coming home. He wrote: "To Ray Billows, Winged Foot means much more than the scene of a championship battle. It means a return to the pastures where fame first rapped on his door and smilingly beckoned to be enveloped. It means the opportunity to show his old friends at Winged Foot that the chance they gave him was not a wasted gesture. Whether Ray wins or loses, every Winged Footer from the club president down to the lowliest caddie will be pulling for their adopted son."

Winged Foot professional Craig Wood liked Ray's chances. "Ray Billows is a grand shotmaker, blessed with an ideal disposition for tournament golf. He never loses his cool and rarely plays a careless shot. His cold nerve counts in the pinches. Bud Ward is a remarkable amateur and Wilford Wehrle has faced the fire of the professionals. But, handsome is as handsome does in golf, and this easily could be Ray Billows' year."

So, the scene was set. Ray was playing very well and was well prepared from a summer of active play. He was playing on one of his favorite courses, one on which he had remarkable success. He would have the enthusiastic support of the galleries, including the throng that surely would make the 60-mile trek from Poughkeepsie. It wasn't implausible even to think that some of the Winged Foot caddies, who loved him from the time he drove into the club in his flivver in 1935, might do something outside the rules to give him an advantage. This could well be the best opportunity that Ray Billows would ever have to win the Amateur.

There was only one problem – Ray Billows was sick. He had come down with a heavy cold, perhaps even the flu, and it was only going to get worse as the week wore on.

Ray qualified for match play with a mediocre score of 153. (The qualifying round included an 83 from a West Coast singer named Bing Crosby.) In his first match, it took him 23 holes to defeat William Dear Jr., when he tied the match on the 18th hole and then won it on the 23rd with a birdie out of a bunker. He seemed to gain strength with sub-par golf to defeat Richard Allman 5&3, but then had to recover from 2-Down after nine holes to prevail over Harry Haverstick on the 19th hole.

Ray was now in the quarterfinals. Waiting for him there was none other than Marvin "Bud" Ward, perhaps the best amateur in the country at the time, and the man who had beaten Ray easily in the final match the year before. It wouldn't be the same this year. Somehow gathering strength, Ray was 4-Up after the first six holes, shot a 1-under-par 35 on the first nine, and went on to beat Ward, 4&3. The victory had to be very satisfying. But, in his typical humble way, Ray called it "a victory for the law of averages."

Ray's semifinal opponent was a self-proclaimed "weekend golfer" from Philadelphia, William B. "Duff" McCullough Jr., who was an underdog coming into the tournament but was playing perhaps his best golf ever. On his way to the semifinals he defeated Willie Turnesa and Johnny Fischer, both former Amateur champions. Ray wasn't himself in his match with McCullough. He could manage only a 76 in the morning round and McCullough's even-par 72 gave him a 4-Up lead. Ray was five over par for the 15 holes played in the afternoon when the match ended with a McCullough win, 5&3. Duff's luck ran out in the final against Dick Chapman, who had defeated Ray's Racine teammate Wilford Wehrle in his semifinal. Chapman became the 1940 Amateur champion convincingly, 11&9.

Ray had to be sorely disappointed and wondering what went wrong. Why couldn't he sustain the form he showed against Ward? Was it bad luck? Was it just destiny for the weekend golfer from Philadelphia? A sportswriter had a different reason: "Ray Billows was in no condition to play golf." It was the wrong time to get sick. Ray would not have had an easy time against Dick Chapman in the final. But he missed a great opportunity to try to win the tournament he wanted most.

Ray's golf year ended with a few local tournaments and then it was time for bowling in the Western Printing league. He rolled an almost perfect game of 278 as part of a 614 series. It was another missed opportunity. It remained to be seen if his plan to retire from major tournaments would be followed.

****

During the year, a second edition of a book titled *Golf as I Play It* was published by Carlyle House. Edited by Richard Chapman and Ledyard Sands, the book features profiles of 28 amateur champions and their comments in various categories of the game, both physical and mental. Ray is included, as are many of the players he faced – Abbott, Chapman, Fischer, Goodman, Holt, Strafaci, Tailer, Turnesa, Wehrle, Yates, etc. The following is a summary of some of Ray's comments.

Most Important Part of Game: The short game – chipping and putting

Strength: Long Irons. Weakness: Putting

Thrill: Being picked for the 1938 Walker Cup Team

Shots to be Remembered: 2-iron to 16th green to set up Eagle 3 when two down with three to play against Jack Creavy in the 1935 New York State Amateur.

Wooden Club Play: Right hand controls the backswing (Only player to say this. 22 say definitely that the left hand controls backswing)

On the Green: Blade Putter, 40 inches long (longest of the 28 players. Shortest is 24 inches, Average is 33 inches)

The Hardest Shot in Golf: Explosion shots when the ball is slightly buried.

Tips and Observations: Concentration and knowing you can do it is the greatest advice I can give for improving anyone's game.

There are curious responses from Ray in the categories of "Shots That Were Missed" and "When Breaks Go Against You." In both cases he refers to his second shot on the 36th hole of his 1937 U.S. Amateur final match against Johnny Goodman and says that the shot was affected by a hidden tree root that restricted his follow-through. As described in Chapter 5, at a dinner in Poughkeepsie after his return from the tournament, Ray said that he "eased up and didn't get through the shot" and conceded that he might have "pressed." Why the different versions? A likely explanation is that, given his humble manner, Ray didn't want to appear to be making excuses in front of a live audience at a dinner and was more comfortable stating the real reason a few years later for a book.

1940 Accomplishments

- Hole In One at Masters
- Low Amateur in Metropolitan Open
- Won his 4th HRGA Championship
- Won the first of six Robert Todd Lincoln Cups
- Won his 3rd New York State Amateur
- Won Eastern Amateur
- Reached the Semifinals of U.S. Amateur

Ray and "Duff" McCullough – 1940 U.S. Amateur Semifinal

9   A Change of Mind

As 1941 began there was something on people's minds other than golf – the developing war in Europe. In February, Ray received a 3A classification from the local Draft Board, a classification that was defined at the time as "Deferred for dependency reasons." It's not fully clear what the reasons were, although Elinor was pregnant at the time. Some of Ray's competitors were not as fortunate. Dick Chapman, Frank Strafaci and Tommy Tailer were on their way to the U.S. Army.

In May, Ray announced his tournament plans for the year, and it seemed clear that the plan he stated the previous fall was for real. The only major tournaments in which he would play were the Metropolitan, New York State and Eastern Amateurs. That left out the Masters, U.S. Open and U.S. Amateur.

The Metropolitan Amateur was played at the Montclair Golf Club in New Jersey in June. On June 11 Ray won medalist honors in the qualifying round with a one-over-par 141 score. There was a far more important occurrence on the same day. Elinor gave birth to their first child, a son who they named Raymond Edward but who became known as Ned. Perhaps it was the excitement of becoming a father, or the effects of traveling back and forth to Poughkeepsie to visit with Elinor and the child, but Ray did not fare well in match play. He lost in the second round to Arthur Lynch, 4&3, after going three-over-par on the front nine.

Ray played better in his next two tournaments but did not win them. He lost in the quarterfinal round of the HRGA Championship to J.W. Leaycraft, 1-Up. Leaycraft went on to win the tournament on his home Rockland Country Club course. Ray then reached the semifinals of the Robert Todd Lincoln Cup but lost to Tommy Pierce, 2-Up.

Things got much better in the Sweetser Victory Cup, which was played at the Sleepy Hollow Country Club in Scarborough, New York. Ray tied the course record with a 67 in the second round, a record held by Jess Sweetser, the man for whom the tournament is named. His 284 total won the tournament, which set another record previously held by Sweetser. Ray's fourth win was the most ever in the event.

Things got even better at the New York State Amateur at the Country Club of Troy. After defeating old foe Tommy Goodwin 1-Up in the semifinals, Ray faced Tommy Pierce for the championship. Pierce was a former Vermont state champion and a member of the home club. He was also the man who defeated Ray in the semifinals of the Robert Todd Lincoln Cup a month earlier. Ray came back from 2-Down after 29 holes to win his fourth New York State title, 1-Up.

An incident that occurred during the match with Pierce illustrates how Ray's personality and conduct on the course made him a favorite of the galleries. A dog ran onto the course during the match and came close to the players. Ray reached out and petted the dog, which he proclaimed to the gallery was for "good luck." For the balance of the match the mutt was "Billows' Dog" to the gallery, and Ray, playing up, didn't forget a friendly pat for the dog after the match.

Poughkeepsie Eagle columnist Ed Rozell made the following comment about the incident: "Ray Billows has that intangible thing called color. He has a personality which reaches out, bridging the chasm between competitor and spectator, to make people want to see him play, to want to see him win. Tommy Pierce, playing on his home course, is a fine fellow and a friendly one, but down the stretch a gallery composed largely of Troy club members was pulling for Ray Billows."

Ray's good play in the Sweetser Victory Cup and New York State Amateur excited him. He decided to change his mind and abandon his plan to not play in the U.S. Amateur. Not only that, but, for the first time ever in his career, he predicted he would win a tournament. Ray Billows proclaimed that it was his time and that he was going to win the National Amateur.

Ray's excitement and optimism did not last very long. At the Metropolitan area qualifying event at Deepdale Golf Club on Long Island, his 36-hole score was a poor 155, which missed qualifying by two strokes. He was out of the U.S. Amateur that he predicted he would win, and he was very disappointed.

A Change of Mind

Then he got a big break. Two of the qualifiers in his area withdrew and he got into the tournament as an alternate. The second of the withdrawals was Bob Jacobson. Apparently, he felt badly for Ray. He said he withdrew because he thought Ray had a good chance to win the tournament while he had next to none.

The site of the Amateur was the Omaha Field Club in Nebraska, nemesis Johnny Goodman's home course. Ray was one of several players who decided to break up the trip to Omaha, as well as get in some extra practice under tournament conditions, by entering the Great Lakes Amateur at the Knollwood Club just outside of Chicago in Lake Forest, Illinois. The posted pairings revealed that Ray would meet Bud Ward in the quarterfinals if they both advanced. They did and a classic "rubber match" was the result. Ward had beaten Ray decisively in the 1939 Amateur final. Ray got revenge the next year with a 4&3 win in the quarterfinals at Winged Foot. Ray bested Ward again at Knollwood. He was two-under-par for the 14 holes he needed for a 5&4 win. He then went on to defeat Art Sweet in the semifinals by a 4&3 margin to set up a championship match with Frank Stranahan.

Frank Stranahan, 19 years old at the time, would become one of the major attractions on the amateur and professional circuits. In a word of the day, he was a "dandy." Frank was rich; he was very good looking; he had a body-builder's body that he maintained until he died at age 90; he wore flashy clothes; he was a magnet for young ladies in the gallery. Frank was also a very good player who was coached by Byron Nelson and who would win many of the major amateur championships, including the Trans-Mississippi, North and South, Western, Canadian and British, as well as six PGA Tour tournaments. He was no match for Ray, who defeated him 6&5 to win the Great Lakes title. Then it was on to Omaha.

Bud Ward had been the clear favorite to win the Amateur. Ray's win in the Great Lakes tournament, including his decisive win over Ward, changed things. Some were now pointing to Ray as the man to beat. The Omaha Field Club caddies had no doubt. Apparently, the Winged Foot caddies had spread word about their hero to their counterparts in Omaha.

Continuing the roller coaster ride that had been the nature of his game for most of the year, Ray barely qualified for match play with a 158 (75, 83). He made it, but his high score placed him low in the pairings where he would meet higher-seeded players in early matches. As it turned out, he won his first two matches relatively easily, 5&3 over Arthur Atkinson and 4&3 over Lloyd Ramsey. It then took a two-under-par performance to overcome Paul White, 3&2, in a difficult match. Ray was now in the quarterfinals, where he met a familiar opponent, Pat Abbott. Pat defeated Ray in the second round at Oakmont in 1938. He did it again in Omaha, 3&2. Ray played just okay at two over par, but he couldn't overcome Pat's one-under-par performance.

Poughkeepsie sportswriter Ed Rozell penned a column titled "Breaks of the Game" after the Amateur. In it he noted two facts. The first was that Pat Abbott was four over par after 18 holes in his semifinal match that followed his win over Ray. The second was that Bud Ward, the man Ray had just beaten in the Great Lakes tournament, ended up winning the Amateur. Rozell posited that with some breaks, or with a different twist of fate, Ray could have been the winner of the tournament that meant the most to him.

Was it the breaks, or fate, or just "golf?" Was it that Ray played less golf than other top amateurs such as Ward, Turnesa, Chapman and others? Whatever it was, Ray had reached the quarterfinals or higher, including two finals, in five of the seven U.S. Amateurs in which he had played. He had won 26 of 33 matches in those tournaments, a remarkable 79 percent. Jess Sweetser, one of the best amateurs ever, claimed that Ray was "consistently the best amateur in the United States." But when was he going to win the damn National Amateur?!

When Ray returned to Poughkeepsie he was treated to yet another dinner. This one was at the Dutchess club in early October with more than half of the membership in attendance. Western Printing president Edward Wadewitz was also present and he revealed the startling news that the company's home plant wanted Ray back in Racine. To the relief of the Dutchess members, he added that Ray would remain in Poughkeepsie "for a while." He also said that the company had given Ray permission to play in the following year's National Amateur.

On December 7, the Japanese attacked Pearl Harbor; the next day the United States declared war on Japan. On December 11, war was declared on Germany and Italy. What effect would World War II have on Ray and amateur golf?

1941 Accomplishments

- Won his 4th Sweetser Victory Cup (a record)
- Won his 4th New York State Amateur
- Won Great Lakes Amateur
- Reached the Quarterfinals of U.S. Amateur

Great Lakes Amateur with Frank Stranahan

1941 - Posing at Dutchess

10   War Years

It didn't take long to find out one significant effect that the United States entry into World War II had on golf. Almost immediately, the USGA cancelled its tournaments for the duration of the war. There would not be another U.S. Open or U.S. Amateur until 1946. The announcement was very disappointing to Ray. He was approaching his 28th birthday and entering an age period during which many golfers reach their prime. He had proven that he was one of the top amateurs in the country and he felt ready to win the major championship that had eluded him, the U.S. Amateur. Now he would have to wait four years to try again.

Ray was not alone. Several of the top amateurs were in the same circumstance. Bud Ward, Willie Turnesa, Johnny Fischer, Dick Chapman, Ted Bishop, Pat Abbott and Wilford Wehrle were all going to be between the ages of 28 and 31 in 1942. Johnny Goodman seemed to be the only "old man" in the group, and he was going to be only 33.

Ray and the others were left to seek out state and regional tournaments that weren't canceled and play in exhibition matches that supported the war effort. As it turned out, a few national tournaments with war-related themes were organized.

In 1942, Ray did not play in a single tournament other than Dutchess club events until July. He did play in an exhibition against professionals Jimmy Thomson and Horton Smith in May at the Southern Dutchess Country Club in Beacon, New York for the benefit of the Red Cross, and in an exhibition at the Hudson River State Hospital course in Poughkeepsie for the benefit of the USO. He considered playing in the Hale America tournament in Chicago. This tournament was played for a single year in 1942 and was considered a war-time substitute for the U.S. Open. The tournament was won by Ben Hogan, which led to an ongoing controversy about whether or not the win represented a record fifth U.S. Open title for Hogan. Ben believed it did; the USGA said it didn't.

Ray did not play in the Hale America because of a business conflict. Although the New York State Amateur was eventually scheduled, at the beginning of the year it was not known if it would be played. The uncertainty may have been a factor in Ray's decision to skip it if it was played and instead play in a new tournament called the All-American Amateur and Open, which was held in Chicago in July. Business reasons again caused a change of plans. Ray decided not to make the trip to Chicago and instead play in the New York State Amateur. Because he had not yet played in a significant tournament, he decided to play in an invitational tournament in Manchester, Vermont as a tune-up. He lost a second-round match.

The New York State Amateur was played at the Niagara Falls Country Club in late July. Despite his lack of competitive play, Ray won medalist honors in the qualifying round with a 67. He advanced to the final when he defeated future professional star Doug Ford, 7&5, in the semifinals. Ray was four-under-par for the 13 holes played, and he called it his best round of golf since 1935. He could not sustain his hot play and lost to Alex Stevenson, a public links player from Niagara Falls, 5&4, in the 36-hole final. It was Ray's second of what would be four runner-up finishes in the New York State Amateur.

Ray's second and final tournament of 1942 was the Chicago National Amateur, played at the Knollwood Club in Lake Forest, Illinois in mid-August. This was the former regional Great Lakes Amateur that Ray won in 1941. It was renamed because it was now national in scope. Ray and his 1941 finals opponent Frank Stranahan were the tournament favorites. Wilford Wehrle was in the field as well. Current U.S. Amateur champion Bud Ward and Western Amateur champion Pat Abbott were in the armed forces and did not compete. Ray was three-under-par for the 47 holes he played in his first three matches, which he won easily. He was upset in the quarterfinals by Mike Stolalik on the 20th hole when he 3-putted. Frank Stranahan was also upset in his quarterfinal match. The tournament was won by Ray's Racine friend Wilford Wehrle, who Ray would have met in the semifinals.

At the start of 1943 Ray was ranked third among Metropolitan Golf Association amateurs. Charlie Whitehead and Bill Dear were ranked first and second. Ray played in only two major tournaments during the year.

The New York State Amateur was played at the Lake Placid Club. Ray advanced easily to the semifinals where he played under-par golf in defeating Jimmie Smith, 6&5. He then won his fifth New York State title by defeating Joe Ruszas, 2&1, in the 36-hole final. The match was all-square after the morning round. Ray went 1-Up on the 27th hole and was never headed.

Ray's other tournament in 1943 was an event organized by the Chicago District Golf Association for the benefit of a fund for wounded veterans of the war. Named the Chicago Victory National, it was a professional-amateur tournament that featured a 36-hole medal play competition among 31 teams comprised of a professional and an amateur, followed by a 72-hole individual medal play competition. The tournament site was the Beverly Country Club in Chicago. Ray's partner for the team competition was supposed to be Gene Sarazen. Gene failed to appear and Ray was paired with Ed Dudley. They finished 11th among the 31 teams. In the individual competition, Ray was tied for the lead in the amateur division after 36 holes with a score of 149. Poor play in the final round led to a score of 79 and a fifth-place finish. The overall individual competition was won by professional Sam Byrd, a former New York Yankees outfielder.

The highlight of 1943 for Ray came in December with the birth of his second child, a six-pound baby girl named Barbara. A *Poughkeepsie Journal* article proclaimed: "It's a darling little blonde in the Ray Billows family."

****

On April 13, 1944 at Fort Dix in New Jersey, Ray Billows was inducted into the United States Army as a Private First Class. He received basic training at Camp Grant, Illinois as part of the Medical Corps. How he ended up with the assignment is the plot of a story that may or not be true or may be partially true.

As the story goes, as a train was about to leave for a basic training site, Ray was pulled from the train by a golf-playing general who recognized Ray's name and his status as one of the country's leading amateurs. Supposedly, the general, seeking help with his golf game, changed Ray's orders from whatever they were to the Medical Corps and routed him to Camp Grant.

It is not known if the general, if there was one, ever got the golf lessons he was seeking. But what is factual is that in September Ray was transferred to Rhoads General Hospital in Utica, New York as an athletic instructor involved with the rehabilitation of wounded soldiers. Given Ray's background, it was an assignment that made sense and was beneficial for Ray.

In July, while on furlough from Camp Grant, Ray entered the Chicago Victory National tournament, an event open to both professionals and amateurs. He did not play well. His 72-hole score of 308 led to a 47th-place finish. The tournament title was shared by professionals Ben Hogan and Jug McSpaden. Ray's army duties prevented him from playing in the 1944 New York State Amateur.

****

In April of 1945, Ray was able get away from his hospital duties to play in a benefit exhibition at the Yahnundasis Golf Club in Utica. He teamed with Ed Furgol, the North and South Amateur champion and a future professional, against Craig Wood, a U.S. Open champion who was paired with a local pro.

In July, he was given permission to play in the New York State Amateur at the Oak Hill Country Club in Rochester. After winning his first two matches easily by 4&3 margins, Ray won close 1-Up matches in the quarterfinal and semifinal matches to advance to the finals against Harry Bill, an Oak Hill member who had played the tournament's best round with a 69 in his semifinal match. Ray built a 4-Up lead in the morning round and went on to defeat Bill, 4&2 to gain his sixth New York State championship.

World War II was ending. By September it would be over. 1946 would bring a return to civilian life for Ray, and a return to national USGA tournaments after a four-year absence.

1942-1945 Accomplishments

- Reached the Finals of New York State Amateur (1942)
- Won his 5th New York State Amateur (1943)
- Won his 6th New York State Amateur (1945)

Ray at Rhoads Rehabilitation Hospital

1946 New York State Amateur – Yahnundasis Golf Club

11   Back in Full Swing

Staff Sergeant Raymond E. Billows was discharged from the United States Army on April 10, 1946. Ray was happy to be back in Poughkeepsie to spend time with Elinor and the children. Ned, now almost five years old, was ready for some golf lessons, and Elinor would welcome some assistance with Barbara, just past her "terrible two" birthday.

Ray was also looking forward to getting back to his Dutchess club to work on his golf game. With a full schedule looming ahead, he was concerned about a sore elbow and the state of his game. In early June he commented that "My game is worse than it's ever been. I'm just a low 80s shooter." He didn't have much time to fix things. The Metropolitan Amateur was only a few weeks away.

The "Met Am" was played at the Essex Country Club in West Orange, New Jersey. Ray played even-par golf and won his first two matches handily by margins of 4&3 and 5&4. He claimed that he had "found his game" by correcting a problem with rolling his wrists. His good play continued in the quarterfinals where he defeated the previous year's runner-up Dom Morano, 4&3. Although he played close to par golf, Ray couldn't get by Doug Ford in the semifinals. The two-time New York Junior champion, and future professional who would win the Masters and PGA tournaments, outlasted him, 2-Up.

As was the case with several other tournaments, the HRGA Championship was not held during the war years. The renewal in 1946 was played at the uniquely named Out O' Bounds Aero and Golf Club in Suffern, New York. Ray tied for medalist honors with James Reynolds and won the medal in a playoff. He went on to win his fifth HRGA title by defeating Reynolds in the final, 3&2.

Ray added another title at the Robert Todd Lincoln Cup in Vermont when he defeated Frank Strafaci in the final, 4&2. The match had to be satisfying to Ray. Strafaci, a former national Public Links champion and five-time Metropolitan Amateur champion, had beaten him in all three of their previous encounters.

Ray's win streak ended at the New York State Amateur, which was played at the Yahnundasis Golf Club in Utica, a course with which Ray was familiar from his time in the army. He reached the semifinals where he defeated Joe Ruszas, 3&2. Ruszas was the defending champion and the man Ray had beaten for the 1943 title. Then it was on to the final against Tommy Goodwin, who defeated Doug Ford in his semifinal match. Ray and Goodwin had met in the state final in 1937 at Oak Hill in Rochester. Ray won that one in a rout, 11&9, but this time the rout went the other way. With a crowd of 1,000 looking on, Ray was 14-over-par for the thirty holes it took Goodwin to win, 8&6. Bad putting was the biggest of Ray's problems. The win was Tommy's third state title. The loss was Ray's third runner-up finish in the event, two of them against Goodwin.

Tommy Goodwin got the best of Ray again in the first post-war edition of the Sweetser Victory Cup. Ray led Tommy by two shots after 36 holes of the 54-hole medal play tournament. Goodwin's 67 in the final round bested Ray's 72 to give him a 208-211 win. It was Goodwin's third title in the event.

Ray's busy golf season continued with two area tournaments. He teamed with his fellow Dutchess member and friend Wes VanBenschoten in the Anderson Memorial at Winged Foot. They lost in the quarterfinals to James Fraser and Bill Hyndman of Atlantic City. Bill Hyndman won numerous amateur and senior amateur titles in an outstanding career.

The Dutchess County Amateur Championship was renewed in 1946 after a 10-year hiatus since its inaugural event. Ray won his second title by defeating Ted Ciferri in the final, 7&6.

The U.S. Amateur was the last major tournament on Ray's 1946 schedule. It was played on a course familiar to him, the Baltusrol Golf Club in Springfield, New Jersey. He tuned up for the tournament by setting a course record score of 67 at the IBM Country Club in Poughkeepsie. When he got to Baltusrol he continued his good play with a one-under-par 143 to qualify for match play. Then something out of the blue happened; Ray lost a first-round match for the first time in the eight National Amateurs in which he had played.

The upset winner was George Hamer, the NCAA champion from the University of Georgia. Ray did not play poorly, but he had only one birdie in a medal score of 74. In an unusual twist, Hamer's medal score was 76, but he had enough good holes for a 1-Up win.

1946 Accomplishments

- Reached the Semifinals of Metropolitan Amateur
- Won HRGA Championship
- Won Robert Todd Lincoln Cup
- Runner-up in New York State Amateur
- Runner-up in Sweetser Victory Cup

****

The new year did not get off to a good start when Ray learned in January that he was not selected for the 1947 Walker Cup team. His reaction was that he was "not surprised but a little disappointed." He spent the winter focused on his job at Western Printing and bowling in the company league, where he had a league-leading 180 average.

Ray's busy tournament schedule continued into 1947, but the results were less than he hoped for. In seeking his sixth title in the HRGA Championship, he tied for medalist honors and managed to advance to the final match. However, he lost to fellow Dutchess member Hank Kowal, 2-Up.

In the New York State Amateur at the Westchester Country Club in Rye, Ray won two matches, including one over his former nemesis Frank Strafaci. He lost in the quarterfinals to Jack Lyons, 2&1, in a match where he was two-over-par and Lyons was even-par.

Ray encountered Jack Lyons again in the quarterfinals of the Met Amateur at the Meadow Brook Club in Westbury, Long Island. Lyons was two-under-par for 15 holes and won, 4&3.

Ray won his only significant tournament of the year in the Sweetser Victory Cup at the Knollwood Country Club in Elmsford, New York. He was tied with Fred Fiore with a score of 215 in the 54-hole event. In the first-ever playoff in the tournament's history, Ray prevailed 75 to 77. It was his fifth Sweetser title.

The 1947 U.S. Amateur was held at the famous Pebble Beach Golf Links on California's Monterey Peninsula. Ray made the trip, although he was bothered by a form of arthritis in his left wrist and elbow. He said he didn't think the problem would affect his play because he "was used to it." It didn't help his play either. He lost a second-round match to Thomas Leonard, 1-Up. Both players shot even-par on the front nine, which ended with the match all-square. Leonard started the back nine 3, 3, 3 (birdie, birdie, par) to take a lead he didn't relinquish.

1947 Accomplishments

- Won Sweetser Victory Cup (fifth title)

****

During 1947 Ray did something he had been thinking about doing for some time; he moved from the city to the country. He found a 150-acre non-working farm in Staatsburg, about 12 miles north of Poughkeepsie. In addition to a large handsome house, the property had two barns, a tenant house and a small cottage. He named the property Riverhill because of its outstanding view of the Hudson River.

Riverhill became a place of relaxation for Ray and his family. He loved to ride around the property on a tractor, just for fun or to mow the fields. The fields were also a wonderful place to hit golf balls; his daughter Barbara was often the caddie who shagged them. Perhaps most of all, Ray enjoyed sitting in a rocking chair on the front porch, looking down at the river. Barbara recalls what the family called "porch time" for family discussions.

12   Third Time a Charm - ?

Ray's hopes for 1948 were focused on bettering his sparse results from the previous year. He did not get an early start on fulfilling those hopes because of business pressures. His first significant tournament of the year was in July at the Robert Todd Lincoln Cup tournament in Vermont. Apparently, his lack of tournament play did not affect his game. He was the medalist and won his third title in the event by defeating Gene Wadsworth in the final, 6&4.

Ray did not play in either the HRGA Championship before the Robert Todd Lincoln Cup or the New York State Amateur after it. When he next played, one of his biggest hopes became a reality – he finally won the Metropolitan Amateur! Ray had tried eight times over eleven years to win the Met Am title, without success. He had played well in the tournament, including a narrow 1-Up loss to George Dunlap in the 1936 final. He continued to play well after 1948. He still holds the record for the most match wins in the tournament, 53, which is three more than Frank Strafaci, who is a 7-time winner of the event.

The 1948 Metropolitan Amateur was played at Winged Foot, the site of several of Ray's successes. His even-par 144 qualifying score was tied for second best. He advanced to the final by playing par or better golf and winning matches handily. His good play continued in the final. He defeated Robert Sweeny, 8&6, for what would be his only Met Amateur title.

As expected, his win caused another party to break out at the Dutchess club. It was called a "Victory Party." The party, of course, celebrated Ray's personal success, but something more as well. There had long been less than a warm relationship between the Metropolitan Golf Association and clubs in the Mid-Hudson Valley. The Dutchess club applied for association membership in 1907, but it was not admitted until 1922 when the mileage requirement for a club to be within 55 miles of New York City was increased to 75 miles. Even after they were admitted, there was a feeling among the "northern clubs" that the association considered them and their players inferior to the clubs and players in the

75

south. Ray's win in the Met Amateur was the first by a member of a northern club, which was reason for celebration at Dutchess. (The relationship with the Met is positive today.)

There was almost another reason to celebrate a win in a Metropolitan event. At the Anderson Memorial, a better-ball-of-partners tournament played at Winged Foot, Ray and Dutchess partner Wes VanBenschoten reached the final when they defeated defending champions Robert Sweeny and Chris Dunphy on the 19th hole in the semifinals. In the final against Ed Vaughn and Bill Schappa, Ray and Wes had a comfortable lead of two up with three holes to play. But, when Schappa birdied #16, Wes missed a 3-foot putt on #17 and Vaughn birdied #18, the match was lost. A Dutchess team has never won the Anderson Memorial.

Ray was playing well and looking forward to the U.S. Amateur, which was played at the Memphis Country Club in Tennessee. The Metropolitan qualifier was at the Deepdale club on Long Island, where Ray's 141 (66-75) qualified easily. The 66 was a Deepdale course record for an amateur, a record that Ray shared with Julius Boros, who would go on to an outstanding professional career that included a U.S. Open championship.

The folks in Poughkeepsie were excited. The win in the Metropolitan Amateur and the record-breaking round at Deepdale had them, as well as Ray, thinking that this could be the year, the third-time-a-charm year, for Ray to win the U.S. Amateur. He was sent off to Memphis with a good-luck scroll signed by virtually every member of the Dutchess club. Among the well-wishers in Poughkeepsie was Ray's dad George, who celebrated his 65th birthday while his son was competing in Memphis.

Another Billows anecdote developed at LaGuardia Airport while Ray waited to board a plane to Memphis. The boarding was being delayed, apparently by a group of press photographers who were waiting for some famous person. When Ray finally went to board, there were shouts of "There he is" and the popping of flashbulbs. The "famous person" they were waiting for was Ray Billows. Unassuming Ray never would have imagined that.

When play started in Memphis, Ray worked his way through wins in five matches, three of which were won comfortably. The

Third Time a Charm -?

other two were difficult matches against very good player Don Schumacher, 2&1, and Michael Cestone, 3&1. In the quarterfinals Ray met the handsome "muscle man" Frank Stranahan, now 26 years old, who was still the darling of the young ladies in the galleries. As he had done at the 1941 Great Lakes Amateur, Ray defeated Stranahan easily, 7&5.

Charlie Coe was Ray's semifinal opponent. 25 years old at the time, Charlie would become a lifetime amateur who was considered one of the best. In the future he would win two U.S. Amateurs, be runner-up in a British Amateur, and be low amateur in three Masters Tournaments. In Memphis he was no match for Ray, who won their match by a 6&5 margin.

Waiting for Ray in the finals was none other than the friend and foe he had met in the late-round and final matches of several Metropolitan, state and national tournaments – Willie Turnesa. Willie, winner of the U.S. Amateur in 1938 and the British Amateur in 1947, defeated former champion Bud Ward in his semifinal match and was the favorite against Ray.

Excitement for the match was high, both in Memphis and in Poughkeepsie. Both players had enthusiastic supporters in the gallery. A contingent of Willie's supporters had flown to Memphis from New York's Westchester County. Ray's friend Wes VanBenschoten, a former Navy pilot, flew a small plane to Memphis on the morning of the match, accompanied by Dutchess members Harry Lyman and Charles Brose. They arrived in time to see the afternoon session. Back in Poughkeepsie, radio station WKIP carried a broadcast of the match. After the match it was reported that the *Poughkeepsie New Yorker* had been flooded with more than 1,000 calls from anxious fans.

An Associated Press article introduced a report of the match with: "It was one of the most fantastic finishes of all the 48 tournaments played, electrifying a crowd of 2,500 that had followed the finalists in a drizzling rain."

The match was described as a "ding-dong wrangle" despite less than stellar play by both players for 27 holes. Turnesa was 1-Up after the morning round with a medal score of 74 versus Ray's 77. Through 27 holes only one birdie had been holed (two were conceded) and Willie led 2-Up. The gallery started to shrink as it sensed a Turnesa victory and fled the rain. But then something happened that had always been a part of Ray's makeup – he battled back. He won the difficult 241-yard 28th hole with a par 3 and knocked in an eagle on the par-five 29th to even the match. As word of the happenings spread, much of the gallery returned. They saw Ray win the 30th with a par to forge ahead, 1-Up. Could this be it? Was the third time to be a charm? Was the 34-year-old, now the "Cinderella Man," finally going to win the National Amateur?

Unfortunately for Ray, and to the disappointment of most in the gallery, the answers were No. Turnesa won the 31st with a par and the 32nd with a birdie to regain the lead. When Ray made bogey on the 33rd and the 34th was halved, Willie was dormie. Both players reached the 35th green in regulation. Ray had a 12-foot putt to keep the match alive. It didn't drop. Ray Billows became the only man to reach the final of the U.S. Amateur three times without winning it. He still is, 68 years later.

It had to be a heart-breaker for Ray, and his wife Elinor stated publicly that it was. He had to lament that just a little bit better play could have given him the title he wanted so badly. But when he returned home to yet another celebratory party at the Dutchess club attended by more than 200 people, his comment was: "I did my best. I have no alibis." It was Ray being Ray.

A year later in an article he wrote for the *USGA Journal*, Ray had this to say about the U.S. Amateur: "Well, somebody has to lose, but why does it always have to be me?" And he laughed. The addition of the laugh was also Ray being Ray.

In the same article he also wrote: "Being a good winner is mighty easy, but it is so important to be a good loser. I guess I've had plenty of practice in the latter, but I will say that, although I've lost the Amateur three times, I've won countless friends with each loss." That too was Ray being Ray, and he was correct about the friends he had won. Soon after the Amateur he received a letter from the great amateur Chick Evans, who said: "I congratulate you who typifies all that the beautiful word loyalty means to the game we love and to friends. You accomplished a great deal in Memphis." It was signed "Your devoted friend."

1948 Accomplishments

- Won Robert Todd Lincoln Cup (third title)
- Won Metropolitan Amateur
- Reached the finals of U.S. Amateur (third time)

****

Despite the loss, reaching the finals of the National Amateur, coupled with winning the Metropolitan Amateur, did have rewards. In the spring of 1949 the USGA announced that Ray Billows was selected as a member of the 1949 Walker Cup team. Locally, he was selected as the Dutchess County Most Outstanding Athlete.

When Ray announced his plans for the year, he sent a mixed message. Unfortunately, it seemed clear that business considerations were having a bigger effect than they ever had. He said: "Back in 1935 and 1936, I had lots of time to practice, but now it's different. The pressures of business prevent me from getting in as much golf as I would like to." On the other hand, he said that he had played his most outstanding golf in 1948, and "I hope to keep on playing for many years. I find that my golf is a tremendous asset as far as my business is concerned."

Where would a golf-work balance be struck? He declined an invitation to play in the Masters because he "was unable to get away at that time." He said he would not play in the Metropolitan Amateur, Metropolitan Open, HRGA and the Dutchess club championship because of business. But he was definitely going to play in the U.S. Amateur at the Oak Hill Country Club, where he had won two of his New York State Amateur titles. He said: "I'm going to play as much weekend golf as I can to get in shape for the tournament. I'd certainly like to win it this time. I've been so close that it's worth another try."

As it turned out, Ray decided to play in the HRGA Championship, where he lost to Hank Kowal in the final, and in the Robert Todd Lincoln Cup, where he was the medalist but lost in the second round. Next was the New York State Amateur at the

Syracuse Yacht and Country Club. Ray won his record seventh championship, which remains the record 67 years later, and may be a record that is never broken. He defeated John Ward in a 39-hole match that could have gone either way. Ward birdied the 36th hole to force extra holes. After both players birdied the 37th hole, Ward missed a 2-foot putt that would have ended the match on the 38th. Ray won on the 39th hole with a par.

Ray broke out a new putter for the U.S. Amateur. Actually, it was an old one that had never been used. The putter was a gift from Charlie Yates. It was made by the famous Scottish clubmaker Tom Stewart of St. Andrews, who made clubs for Old Tom Morris, Harry Vardon and Bob Jones. The club, which was a blade type versus the mallet type Ray had been using, had "sat in a corner" of his home for eleven years. Ray's comment about the putter change is revealing: "I think that every important tournament I've lost can be traced to putting." More about that comment later.

Ray's play at Oak Hill was not his best. He did win his first match easily, 7&5, against L. William Eisenmann. But, he had to come back from two holes down to beat Eugene Bates in a match that went to the 20th hole, and he won a close match over Kenneth Corcoran, 2-Up. His fourth-round opponent was a familiar one, Willie Turnesa, the friend who had narrowly defeated him in the previous year's final. It wasn't close this time; Willie won, 6&5. Ray's post-match comment reflected his less-than-best play: "I should have lost before I did."

The year ended on a positive note in the Walker Cup Match at Winged Foot. Unlike Ray's first Walker Cup when the U.S. team lost for the first time, the American team was dominant in a 10-2 victory. Ray and Willie Turnesa, which was the #1 American team, played in the foursomes matches against Englishman Ronnie White and Irishman Joe Carr. White and Carr won, 3&2, for the only British foursomes win. In the singles Ray defeated Ken Thom of England, 2&1.

A comment made by Ray at the end of the year reflected his continuing ardent desire to win the National Amateur: "I will continue to play in the Amateur as long as I can." The last five words in the comment are revealing, and ominous. Ray was now 35 years old. He was still a young man, but he was approaching old age in golfing years. As it turned out, he would play in only four more Amateurs, and he would not get to the quarterfinals in any of them. Further, his win in the New York State Amateur was his last win in that tournament.

What did the future hold for Ray Billows?

1949 Accomplishments

- Selected for Walker Cup Team (1-1 record)
- Won New York State Amateur (record 7th time)

Ray at Dutchess with Walker Cup

1947 at Dutchess
Ray and Elinor with Gloria Garlick and Bill Bogle

13   Changes in the 1950s

Ray Billows entered the 1950s at age 35. When he left the decade ten years older, he had, for the most part, left the limelight of the national scene of amateur golf. He continued to play in local, area and state tournaments, and had some success. But increased business pressure brought on by a job promotion, a change in personal focus, as well as advancing age, affected both his participation and his performance.

There were signs of things to come in 1950. Because of business activity, Ray declined a Masters invitation and did not play in the New York State Amateur. He announced that he would try to qualify for the U.S. Open and National Amateur. As it turned out, he had a very active schedule for the year.

He missed qualifying for the U.S. Open with a poor 153 score, but he played well in local and area tournaments. He won the HRGA Championship for the sixth time by defeating Dutchess member Hank Kowal in the final, 5&4. He won the Robert Todd Lincoln Cup for the fourth time with a 2&1 win over Pierce Russell, the defending champion. Ray played well in two Metropolitan Golf Association events. In the Met Amateur he reached the semifinals, where he lost to old nemesis Frank Strafaci, 2&1. In the Met Open he was the low amateur.

Ray qualified for the National Amateur but lost in the first round for only the second time. His opponent at the Minneapolis Golf Club was 21-year-old Gene Littler, a player who would go on to an outstanding professional career that included a U.S. Open championship. Gene bested Ray, 6&4. In other tournament action, Frank Stranahan defeated a 20-year-old future "king" named Arnold Palmer on his way to the finals, where he lost to Sam Urzetta in a 39-hole match. (Palmer won the Amateur in 1954.)

In local action, Ray won his seventh Dutchess club title and lowered his Dutchess course record to 65.

The only tournament Ray won in 1951 was his fifth Robert Todd Lincoln Cup. He reached the third round of the New York State Amateur but failed to qualify for the National Amateur. In

83

the Amateur qualifier an 82 in the second round did him in.

Results were better in two 1952 tournaments. In the New York State Amateur at Wolferts Roost Country Club in Albany, Ray defeated three-time champion Tommy Goodwin in the quarterfinals and reached the final match against defending champion Bill Shields. Poor play led to an 8-over-par medal score and a 6&5 loss to Shields. It was Ray's last appearance in a New York Amateur final.

Prior to the start of the National Amateur at the Seattle Golf Club in Washington, Ray talked about the uncertainty of 18-hole match play and the luck that is often involved, and he also discussed the chances of various players. With respect to his own chances he said: "Even I might get lucky." When play started it looked like he just might get lucky. After a first-round bye, he came back from 3-Down after nine holes to defeat George Beechler, 1-Up, and then won over Roy Moe Jr., 2-Up. His luck ran out against University of Washington student Paul Johanson when he went 8-over-par in losing, 5&3.

An August, 1953 article in the *Poughkeepsie Journal* summed up the year concisely, and ominously: "This is the first year in many that Ray Billows hasn't won a major golf crown, or even come close." Ray did not qualify for either the U.S. Open or the National Amateur. A score of 160 failed in the Open; a 153 at his favorite Winged Foot course failed in the Amateur. He lost in the second round of three tournaments: the Robert Todd Lincoln Cup, the Metropolitan Amateur, and the Anderson Memorial. The only good news was setting two course records, a 64 at Dutchess and a 62 at the Southern Dutchess Country Club in nearby Beacon, New York. Ray called the 62 "as good as any round I have ever played."

During 1953 Ray received a significant promotion at Western Printing. He was named the Eastern Regional Sales Manager. By the end of the year, he claimed: "I'm just a weekend golfer."

1954 was another mediocre year for Ray. He bypassed the New York State Amateur for the Robert Todd Lincoln Cup and won it for the sixth time. However, he failed to qualify for the U.S. Open with a 36-hole score of 159, and the U.S. Amateur with a score of 154. He reached the quarterfinals of the Metropolitan Amateur, where he lost to seven-time champion Frank Strafaci, 6&4. Ray had a local highlight when he broke the course record at The Powelton Club in Newburgh, New York with a 65 during a HRGA team event.

Ray's son Ned showed some interest in golf at an early age and developed some skill as an adult. However, he never had a real dedication to the game. In a Father-Son event at Dutchess in 1954 when he was 13 years old, Ned shot 123 with a handicap of 40 for a net score of 83. Ray's net score of 67 wasn't enough to help the team. Ned was just getting started in golf at the time.

The only 1955 highlight for Ray came at the National Amateur at the Country Club of Virginia in Richmond. After a first-round 1-Up win over young star Don Bisplinghoff, Ray remarked that "I never worked so hard in my life." Apparently, he continued to work hard to get to the fourth round. However, when he got there he didn't win a hole against Hillman Robbins and lost, 9&7.

The last four years of the 1950s were much the same as the first six – a mixture of failed qualifiers for the U.S. Open, U.S. Amateur and Metropolitan Amateur, failure to advance very far when he did qualify in these events and in the New York State Amateur, increasingly inconsistent scoring with some high numbers that were rare in earlier years, and some success locally, including another record round of 64 at Dutchess, three club championships, and a low-amateur and third-place overall finish in a new pro-am event named The Mid-Hudson Open.

1959 was the last year in which Ray played in the U.S. Amateur. In 15 Amateurs he played in 59 matches and won 44 of them, a remarkable 74.6 winning percentage.

There was an interesting sidelight to the 1959 Amateur at the Broadmoor Club in Colorado Springs. A youngster from Ohio State University defeated defending champion Charlie Coe in the final, 1-Up. The youngster's name was Jack Nicklaus. A new era in golf had begun.

Some things Ray said in 1957 explain where he was golf-wise at the time and where he was headed. He said that he was now playing golf for fun. Family members were now part of his trips to some tournaments – Elinor and daughter Barbara were with him in Elmira for the 1957 New York State Amateur. As he put it, "I go where I'm going to have fun rather than just play golf."

The following quote was the most telling: "I can't seem to rise to the occasion like I once did, except for the National Amateur. And I'm getting too old for that, too."

Ray Billows would reach the age of 46 in 1960.

1953
Western Printing Eastern Regional Sales Manager

14   Winding Down

The years in Ray's life from 1960 to 1990 were a combination of a winding down of the competition level of the tournaments in which he played and a meaningful change in his personal life. By 1970, at age 56, he had stopped trying to qualify for national and Metropolitan Golf Association tournaments. His last attempt to qualify for the U.S. Amateur was in 1969. In 1965, when the tournament format was changed to medal play, Ray commented that he doubted that he would reach the finals again. His dream of winning the Amateur would not become reality. He continued to try to qualify for a few years only so he could have a reunion with his former competitors and friends.

Ray did not stop playing golf. He started playing in the Senior events of the New York Golf Association and the Dutchess club. He also added some new local tournaments such as the Westchester Golf Association Amateur and the Dutchess County Amateur, and he continued to play in invitational and member-guest events at several clubs.

While the winding down was taking place, there were some highlights, some "epiphanies" so to speak. He reached the quarterfinals of the Metropolitan Amateur in 1962 and the finals in 1966. The 1966 event was at the Inwood Country Club on Long Island. Ray's opponent was Jimmy Fisher, who really got the jump on him in the final match – Jimmy was 6-Up after nine holes. Ray made another of his comebacks to get to 2-Down after 26 holes. But, he didn't win another hole and lost, 5&3.

In 1963, Ray reached the fourth round of the New York State Amateur at the Knollwood Country Club in Elmsford. In the second round he came back from 4-Down to win. He lost to Lloyd Ribner in the fourth round, 4&3. Ray was disappointed with the loss mostly because he was looking forward to playing against his old friend and opponent Tommy Goodwin. He commented: "The way things are going, it may have been our last chance." Ray made one final attempt at the New York Amateur in 1972 when it was played at Dutchess. At age 58, he missed the cut with scores of 80 and 78.

In Senior competition Ray won several championships, including those of the Westchester Golf Association and Dutchess County, as well as five Senior titles at his Dutchess club. The highlight was winning the New York State Senior title in 1974.

Ray won the last of his record 14 Dutchess club championships in 1965. He continued to compete for the championship for several years; he reached the final in 1974.

Ray had another highlight at the Dutchess club. In 1984 at age 70, he shot a 68, which what was thought to be the first time in the club's history that someone had shot their age or better. His handicap was five at the time. His comments about the achievement are indicative of his humility and good humor. "I don't shoot those all the time. The other day I shot a 75 and people were congratulating me for shooting my age. I was highly insulted."

There were two other golf-related happenings of note during Ray's winding down period. In 1960 he became somewhat of a golf course architect in a partnership of sorts with Gene Sarazen. At the time, the Dinsmore Golf Course, a public course in Ray's home town of Staatsburg, was being expanded to 18 holes. The original course dates to 1893 as a 9-hole private course of wealthy Hudson River families. Sarazen, who owned a fruit tree farm in nearby Germantown and played the original course with Ray, took an interest in the project. Hal Purdy was the official architect. The roles of Gene and Ray were explained by the commissioner of the Taconic Park Commission, which operated the course: "Gene is directing, free of charge, the job of transferring the Dinsmore course into an 18-hole layout. We are giving him pretty much a free hand and he is having the time of his life. He wants the grass to be greener, the sand to be whiter and the flags to be more vivid than any other course in the country. When he comes down, Ray Billows often joins him and they have a wonderful time planning and playing."

In 1979, Ray had a warm reunion with Willie Turnesa, one of his old friends in a 40-year rivalry. Willie was playing in his first

New York State Senior tournament, which was held at the Dutchess club. His comments suggest that he played in the event because it was an opportunity to see Ray again. He said: "We had a good time talking about yesteryear. There's some sort of a fraternity among golfers. Ray is one of the nicest people I've known, and he loves to play golf." In an unimportant sidelight for both of them, Ray won the Class B (ages 65-70) division of the tournament by three strokes over Willie.

Willie Turnesa knew what he was saying when he said that Ray "loves to play golf." Like so many of us who play the game, Ray was dedicated to improving his game by searching for and tinkering with new ideas and believing they would work. In an interview in 1972, a year in which he hadn't won anything of significance, he remarked: "It's too bad the season is over. I'm playing better than I have in years and with lots of confidence." He went on to say that after always being a natural hooker, he was now playing left to right, and that he had changed to putting cross-handed and "believe me, I have never putted better."

In 1984 at age 70 Ray was playing golf at Dutchess three times a week. In nine years he wouldn't be playing at all.

****

Significant changes occurred in Ray's personal life during the winding down period. He retired from Western Printing in 1969 after a 35-year career. His regional sales manager job began to require him to spend more time in New York City, something he did not like to do. In the same year, the first of his four grandchildren was born, which added a new dimension to his life that he enjoyed very much.

Ray's father George died in 1970 at age 88. His stepmother Helen moved back to her native Racine after George's death; she died there in 1974 at age 85.

The biggest impact came in 1978 when his beloved redhead Elinor died. She was diagnosed with cancer in 1971. She confronted the disease bravely and stoically and appeared to be fighting it successfully; but the cancer returned. Elinor's funeral took place in a Presbyterian church. The promise made by Ray and Elinor to work things out with respect to their different religions was kept.

After Elinor's death Ray became somewhat of a loner, but not for very long. Jim and Winnie Peelor repeated what they had done forty years earlier – they "set up" Ray with a woman, this time at a dinner party they hosted. The woman was somebody Ray knew, Carolyn (Lynn) VanBenschoten. Lynn's husband Wes, who competed with Ray at Dutchess and was his partner in the Anderson Memorial, died in 1978, the same year and in the same week of Elinor's death. Ray and Lynn were married in 1981. Ray sold the Riverhill property and moved into Lynn's house in Poughkeepsie.

It's noteworthy that two women Ray loved each made an impact on his life at the time of their death. On her deathbed, his mother Clara had him make a promise to attend Sunday Mass, a promise he kept throughout his life. Before his wife Elinor died she worried about his future and encouraged him to remarry.

15   Final Years

Ray began to have health problems in the 1980s, especially with his hips, and with his back as well. By 1990 both hips had been replaced, which had the expected effect of limiting his ability to play golf. In 1993 his left hip was giving him further discomfort and he underwent another operation. It was the first year in a very long time in which he did not play a single round of golf.

Ray kept trying to play. In a 1994 newspaper interview he mentioned that he tried to hit a few balls in the backyard and "Boy, it was like murder." About not being able to play, he said: "I miss it. It is the only thing I really did with my spare time. I lay in bed at night, bad hip and all. I reminisce and think back of the matches I have played and the people I have met and all the good things that have happened to me because of golf."

Ray spent most of his time watching television, especially golf. (He was especially impressed with Tiger Woods.) For the most part, the only time he left his house was to go to church on Sundays to pray that his hips would get better.

He didn't give up. In April, 2000 Ray entered St. Francis Hospital in Poughkeepsie for another hip repair operation. When he was given anesthesia his blood pressure dropped precipitously and the operation was postponed. Two days later, while still in the hospital, his heart failed. The Cinderella Kid was dead at age 85, two months before his 86th birthday.

As they had done often when Ray returned from tournaments, the members of the Dutchess club turned out for Ray's funeral at St. Mary's Catholic Church in Poughkeepsie. The central part of the ceremony was the Funeral Mass. Somehow, it seemed as though Ray's mother Clara was there – and Elinor as well.

*New York State Golf Association
Hall of Fame – Inaugural Class*

Epilogue

On November 10, 2012, Ray Billows was inducted into the newly created New York State Golf Association Hall of Fame as part of its inaugural class. A large crowd attended the event at the Oak Hill Country Club in Rochester, a club at which Ray won two of his record seven New York State Amateur Championships. I had the privilege of making the introductory remarks related to Ray. When the program concluded, I and Ray's daughter Barbara were approached by several people whose initial words were largely "I didn't know," followed by complimentary remarks about Ray. I spoke with Don Allen, another inductee who won six state titles, and asked him if he knew Ray. He said: "Not really, but that's one helluva record."

It occurred to me that how could most of the attendees know about Ray Billows. It had been almost eighty years since he burst onto the amateur golf scene at Winged Foot. As for Don Allen's comment, yes, certainly it is one helluva record. The primary purpose of this book is to let the golf world of the present and future know about that record and, just as importantly, about the man who created it.

A nagging question is how to consider Ray's record against other golf accomplishments. The starting point must be that Ray was not able to win the U.S. Amateur. Why? How could someone good enough to win 75% of his matches, reach the fourth round or better in 9 of 15 events, including the final round three times, not win? Further, Ray was the only player to reach the final three times in the period from 1930 to 1950.

In a 1999 article in the *USGA Journal* titled "A Great Amateur," author Andrew Armstrong raises the question of whether it was bad golf or bad luck, and answers the question by saying, in large part, that it was bad timing. He points out that the first finals loss, when Ray was 23 years old, came on the 36th hole to Johnny Goodman, an experienced player who had won the U.S. Open as an amateur; the second loss was to Marvin "Bud" Ward, an outstanding amateur who was enjoying his best year in golf, had made the lowest score ever by an amateur in the U.S. Open earlier in the year, and was twelve under par for the 103 holes he played coming into the match with Ray; the third loss came on the 35th hole to Willie Turnesa, who already had won both a U.S. and a British Amateur.

Armstrong also mentions that, except for Goodman, Ray eventually defeated every leading amateur to whom he had lost, most of them more than once, including Bud Ward and Willie Turnesa. So, timing does seem to be a factor in the finals losses.

Three additional factors can be mentioned, two related to bad luck and one related to golf. Perhaps Ray's best chance to win the Amateur was in 1940 at his favorite Winged Foot where he lost in a semifinal upset during a week during which he was afflicted with a heavy cold that led a sportswriter to write that "Ray Billows was in no condition to play golf." It was also unlucky that World War II caused a suspension of the Amateur from 1942 to 1945, four years during which Ray was in the prime playing years of ages 28 to 31.

As for golf, Ray's inconsistent putting was sometimes what kept him from winning more than he did. He once said: "I think that every important tournament I've lost can be traced to putting." He was rarely a poor putter, but too often he didn't have as many one-putt greens as his opponents.

There are other things to be considered with respect to both the record and the man. Much like Johnny Goodman, Ray came from far less than a privileged background. His rise to the highest levels of amateur golf was from caddie to shipping clerk to "Cinderella Man." His business career as a salesman, and eventually as a sales executive, clearly impacted his practice time and the extent of his tournament participation. Simply put, he did not practice as much or play as much tournament golf as many of his contemporaries.

The Cinderella moniker that stayed with Ray throughout his career reflects a perception of him as an underdog. That perception, plus his many stirring comebacks, plus his colorful and humble personality, made him a favorite of both galleries and the press, which, in turn, created enthusiasm for amateur golf.

The best reflection of Ray Billows the man is how he dealt with golf's cruel companions of frustration and heartbreak, most especially with respect to the U.S. Amateur title that he never won. He met defeat with grace and an uncommon level of sportsmanship, and with humor as well. He was quick to extend his hand to a winning opponent, and always with a smile on his face. In another magazine article that focused on the three defeats in the U.S. Amateur final, he said: "Being a good winner is mighty easy, but it is so important to be a good loser. I guess I've had plenty of practice in the latter."

So, yes, certainly it is "a helluva record," as a competitor, as a gentleman, and as a representative of amateur golf. And, yes, as Bob Jones said, "It's a rotten shame for us so readily to overlook the fine fellows and the truly great golfers who for one reason or another never have got within that charmed circle of national championship."

Charlie Yates captured Ray Billows perfectly when he said:

> "To me, he exemplifies what amateur golf is all about. He is both a great amateur and a great gentleman."

****

Appendix

RAY BILLOWS
MAJOR ACHIEVEMENTS

Milwaukee District Amateur Champion	1934
International Open Amateur Champion	1937
Eastern Amateur Champion	1940
Great Lakes Amateur Champion	1941
Metropolitan Amateur Champion	1948
Metropolitan Open – Low Amateur	2 Times
Sweetser Victory Cup Champion	5 Times (Record)
Robert Todd Lincoln Cup Champion	6 Times (Record)
New York State Amateur Champion	7 Times (Record)
New York State Senior Champion	1974
USGA National Amateur Finalist (Match Record: 44-15 = 74.6%)	1937, 1939, 1948
United States Walker Cup Team	1938, 1949
Masters Tournament Participant	1939, 1940
Hudson River Golf Association Champion	6 Times
Dutchess Golf and Country Club Champion	11 Times

Dutchess County Golf Hall of Fame
Racine County Sports Hall of Fame
Wisconsin Golf Association Hall of Fame
New York State Golf Association Hall of Fame

U.S. AMATEUR RECORD

Year	Matches Won	Round Lost In	Opponent	Match Result
1935	2	3	Fred Haas Jr.	2 & 1
1936	5	QF	Johnny Goodman	2 & 1
1937	6	Final	Johnny Goodman	2 Up
1938	1	2	Pat Abbott	2 & 1
1939	5	Final	Marvin (Bud) Ward	7 & 5
1940	4	SF	W.B. McCullough Jr.	5 & 3
1941	3	QF	Pat Abbott	1 Up
1946	0	1	George Hamer Jr.	1 Up
1947	1	2	Thomas Leonard Jr.	1 Up
1948	7	Final	Willie Turnesa	2 & 1
1949	3	4	Willie Turnesa	6 & 5
1950	0	1	Gene Littler	6 & 4
1952	3	4	Paul Johnson	5 & 3
1955	3	4	Hillman Robbins Jr.	9 & 7
1959	1	2	Dr. Arthur Butler	4 & 2

44   Matches Won Percentage: 44 / 59 = 74.6%

NEW YORK STATE AMATEUR CHAMPIONSHIPS

Year	Club	Finals Opponent	Margin
1935	Winged Foot West	Jack Creavy	37 Holes
1937	Oak Hill	Tommy Goodwin	11 & 9
1940	Onondaga	Willie Turnesa	8 & 6
1941	CC of Troy	Tommy Pierce	1 Up
1943	Lake Placid	Joe Ruszas	2 & 1
1945	Oak Hill	Harry Bill Jr.	4 & 2
1949	Syracuse Yacht	John Ward	39 Holes

Between 1935 and 1954, Ray played in 15 championships. He reached the semifinals or higher in 13 of them.

U.S. AMATEUR CHAMPIONS – 1930 to 1950

Year	Champion	Runner-Up	Margin
1930	Robert T. Jones	Eugene Homans	8 & 7
1931	Francis Ouimet	Jack Westland	6 & 5
1932	C. Ross Somerville	Johnny Goodman	2 & 1
1933	George Dunlap Jr.	Max Marston	6 & 5
1934	Lawson Little Jr.	David Goldman	8 & 7
1935	Lawson Little Jr.	Walter Emery	4 & 2
1936	Johnny Fischer	Jack McLean	37 Holes
1937	Johnny Goodman	**Ray Billows**	2-Up
1938	Willie Turnesa	Pat Abbott	8 & 7
1939	Marvin "Bud" Ward	**Ray Billows**	7 & 5
1940	Richard Chapman	W.B. McCullough Jr.	11 & 9
1941	Marvin "Bud" Ward	Pat Abbott	4 & 3
-------------	1942-1945: No Tournament – WWII	-------------	
1946	Stanley Bishop	Smiley Quick	37 Holes
1947	Skee Reigel	John Dawson	2 & 1
1948	Willie Turnesa	**Ray Billows**	2 & 1
1949	Charles Coe	Rufus King	11 & 10
1950	Sam Urzetta	Frank Stranahan	39 Holes

THE AMATEURS

The following are brief summaries of the records of several of the amateurs against whom Ray Billows competed, including the winners of the U.S. Amateur from 1930 through 1950.

Pat Abbott (1912-1984): Pat was born in Pasadena, California. His amateur championships include the 1935 Southern California Open, the 1936 U.S. Amateur Public Links, the 1938 and 1941 Southern California Amateur, and the 1942 Western Amateur. He played in only four U.S. Amateurs but advanced to the finals twice, where he lost to Willie Turnesa in 1938 and to Bud Ward in 1941. Pat turned professional after World War II and served as the head professional at Memphis Country Club for 34 years. He won the Tennessee Open four times and the Tennessee PGA Senior Championship three times. He was inducted into the Tennessee Golf Hall of Fame in 2002.

Stanley "Ted" Bishop (1913-1986): In 1946 when the U.S. Amateur resumed after WWII, Ted won the tournament in a 37-hole final match against Smiley Quick. A native New Englander from Natick, Massachusetts, he won three Massachusetts Amateurs and two New England Amateurs. He was a member of winning Walker Cup teams in 1947 and 1949.

Dick Chapman (1911-1978): Dick was a native of Greenwich, Connecticut and a member of Winged Foot when he won the U.S. Amateur at his home club in 1940. In the final he defeated W.B. McCullough Jr., the man who had upset Ray Billows in the semifinals. Dick also won the 1951 British Amateur. His amateur titles included state championships in New York, Connecticut, Massachusetts, and the Carolinas. He won the Canadian Amateur, the North and South Amateur and the New England Amateurs. Dick competed in fourteen U.S. Amateurs; in addition to his win in 1940, he reached the quarterfinals in 1957. He was a member of winning Walker Cup teams in 1947, 1951 and 1953.

Charlie Coe (1923-2001): Charlie is considered one of the best amateur golfers ever. A lifetime amateur, he won the U.S. Amateur in 1947 and 1958, and was runner-up to Jack Nicklaus in 1959. He also won the Western Amateur and four Trans-Mississippi Amateurs. He reached the finals of the British Amateur in 1951. He played on six Walker Cup teams and served as captain twice. Charlie played in 19 Masters Tournaments. He was the low amateur in the tournament six times, including titles in four consecutive decades from the 1940s to the 1970s. In 1961 he finished second overall, one stroke behind Gary Player. A native of Ardmore, Oklahoma, Charlie served as a pilot in WWII and had a career in the oil business. In 1964 he received the USGA's Bob Jones Award in recognition of distinguished sportsmanship in golf.

George Dunlap Jr. (1908-2003): The son of the co-founder of Grossett & Dunlap Publishers, George was introduced to golf at age three when his father purchased a tiny blade putting cleek for him at the Wanamakers Department Store in New York City. George graduated from Princeton in 1931. While at the university he won the Intercollegiate Individual Championship in 1930 and 1931 and led Princeton to the team championship in 1930. He won the Long Island Amateur in 1932 and seven North-South Amateurs between 1931 and 1942. He was a semi-finalist in the British Amateur in 1933 and 1934. In 1936 he bested Ray Billows, 1-Up, for the New York Metropolitan Amateur title. George was a member of three winning Walker Cup teams in 1932, 1934 and 1936.

Johnny Fischer (1912-1984): Johnny was born in Cincinnati, Ohio. As a student at the University of Michigan, he won three individual Big Ten Conference Championships and, in 1932, the NCAA Championship. In nine U.S. Amateur appearances he reached the quarterfinals twice, the semifinals once, and won the championship in 1936 in a 37-hole match against Jack McLean. Johnny played on the 1934, 1936 and 1938 Walker Cup teams, and was the captain of the 1965 team.

Johnny Goodman (1909-1970): Perhaps best known as the last amateur to win the U.S. Open, which he won in 1933, Goodman rose from an orphaned childhood in Omaha, Nebraska to become one of the best American amateurs. A 3-time winner of the Nebraska and Trans-Mississippi Amateurs, he captured national attention when, at age 19, he upset Bob Jones in the first round of the 1929 U.S. Amateur at Pebble Beach. It took him nine tries before he finally won the U.S. Amateur in 1937 in a close final match against Ray Billows. Johnny played on the 1934, 1936 and 1938 Walker Cup teams. He turned professional in 1960 after supporting himself throughout most of his career by selling insurance.

Chuck Kocsis (1913-2006): Like Johnny Fischer, Kocsis excelled at the University of Michigan. He was a member of two NCAA Championship teams and the individual NCAA Champion in 1936. Chuck won six Michigan State Amateurs and three Michigan Opens; he was named the Michigan amateur golfer of the century and is a member of the Michigan Golf Hall of Fame. On the national stage, Chuck competed in fourteen U.S. Amateurs. He reached the quarterfinals twice and the 1956 final, where he lost to E. Harvie Ward Jr. He was the low amateur in two U.S. Opens and two Masters Tournaments, and a member of the 1938, 1949 and 1957 Walker Cup teams.

Lawson Little (1910-1968): Before turning professional in 1936 and winning eight professional titles, including the 1936 Canadian Open and the 1940 U.S. Open, Lawson had an outstanding amateur career. He won both the U.S. and British Amateurs in 1934 and 1935; he is the only player to win both titles in the same year twice. He was the low amateur in the U.S. Open in 1934, the low amateur in both the Masters and British Open in 1935, and a member of a winning Walker Cup team is 1934. An interesting sidelight: Lawson often carried 26 clubs in his bag. He was likely a contributor to the USGA's 14-club limit that was established in 1938.

Skee Riegel (1914-2009): A Pennsylvania native, Skee played baseball and football in college but did not take up golf until age 23. He won the U.S Amateur in 1947 at Pebble Beach and was a member of the 1947 and 1949 Walker Cup teams. He became a professional in 1950. Skee played in 11 consecutive Masters from 1947 to 1957; he finished second to Ben Hogan in 1951. He became a club professional in 1954.

Ross Somerville (1903-1991): A Canadian from London, Ontario, Ross was both a champion golfer and an all-around athlete. He won six Canadian Amateur championships between 1926 and 1937. He also won four Canadian Senior championships in the 1960s. In 1932 he became the first Canadian to win the U.S. Amateur. At the University of Toronto, he played football and ice hockey. He was also one of Canada's top cricket players and an Olympian. Ross served as president of the Royal Canadian Golf Association in 1957. He is a member of several Canadian sports halls of fame.

Frank Strafaci (1916-1988): Born and raised in Brooklyn, New York, Frank was a dominant player among the traditionally strong amateurs in the New York metropolitan area. He won the Metropolitan Amateur a record seven times and the Long Island Amateur five times. Nationally, he won the North and South Amateur twice and was the U.S. Public Links Champion in 1935. Frank had only modest success in the U.S. Amateur. In sixteen appearances, he won 26 matches (62%); he reached the round of sixteen four times and the quarterfinals twice.

Frank Stranahan (1922-2013): Dubbed the "Toledo Strongman" because of his dedication to powerlifting, Frank had success both as an amateur and a professional. The highlights of his amateur career were British Amateur Championships in 1948 and 1950. He won 49 other amateur titles, including the Western (4), North and South (3), Canadian (2), Mexican (2), Great Lakes (2) and Trans-Mississippi (1). As an amateur he finished second in The Open (British) twice and in the Masters Tournament once. He was a member of three winning Walker Cup teams (1947, 1949 and

1951). His dream of winning the U.S. Amateur was not realized. In nine appearances, he reached the quarterfinals once and lost a 39-hole match to Sam Urzetta in the 1950 final. Frank became a professional in 1954 at the age of 32. He won four PGA Tour events as an amateur and two more as a professional.

Jess Sweetser (1902-1989): Most of Sweetser's success as a player came in the 1920s, but he remained active in amateur golf for many years. Jess won the NCAA Individual Championship as a Yale student in 1920. In 1922 he won the U.S. Amateur when he defeated Bob Jones, 8&7, in the semifinals and Chick Evans, 3&2, in the final. In the 11 Amateurs in which he played, he reached another final in 1923, a semifinal in 1930, and three quarterfinals. In 1926 at Muirfield he became the first American-born player to win the British Amateur (Walter Travis, a naturalized American born in Australia, won the title in 1904.) Jess was a member of the original Walker Cup team in 1922, and also played in 1923, 1924, 1926, 1928 and 1932. He was the non-playing captain in 1967 and 1973. He served as treasurer and on the executive committee of the USGA. In 1986 he received the USGA's Bob Jones Award winner in recognition of distinguished sportsmanship in golf.

Willie Turnesa (1914-2001): Ray Billows' good friend Willie lived in Elmsford, New York for most of his life. His illustrious amateur career included two U.S. Amateur titles (1938, 1948) and a British Amateur title (1947). He also won the New York State Amateur and the Metropolitan Amateur and was runner-up in another British Amateur. His widely-recognized skill as a player is reflected by the courses on which he won two of his major titles – Oakmont in the 1938 U.S. Amateur and Carnoustie in the 1947 British Amateur. He played on three consecutive winning Walker Cup teams in 1947, 1949 and 1951; he was the playing captain on the 1951 team. Willie was dedicated to golf in his home area. He co-founded the Westchester Golf Association Caddie Scholarship Fund in 1956, which is his enduring legacy. He was prouder of the caddie scholarship fund than any of his championships.

Sam Urzetta (1926-2011): Sam is a member of the Hall of Fame at Saint Bonaventure University. He was the captain of the school's basketball team and led the nation in free throw percentage during his junior year. An outstanding athlete, he turned to amateur golf after college and rose quickly in the national ranks. He won the New York State Amateur in 1948 and the U.S. Amateur in 1950 in a 39-hole finals match against Frank Stranahan. He was a member of winning Walker Cup teams in 1951 and 1953. Sam turned professional in 1954. After a brief stint on the professional tour, in 1956 he became the club pro at the prestigious Country Club of Rochester in his New York home town. He served at CCR for 38 years.

Marvin "Bud" Ward (1913-1968): Ward and Willie Turnesa are the only Ray Billows' contemporaries to win two U.S. Amateurs, one of which for both was over Ray in the final. In nine U.S. Amateur appearances, Bud reached the quarterfinals or better in four of them. He also won three Western Amateurs, two Washington State Amateurs and a Pacific Northwest Amateur. He was a Walker Cup team member in 1938 and 1947. Ward turned professional in 1949. He worked as a club pro and played in regional tournaments until his 1968 death from cancer.

Wilford Wehrle (1914-1991): Ray Billows' high school teammate was ranked as the #3 amateur in the U.S. in 1938, a ranking achieved with only one win of national significance, the 1937 Western Open (in which he defeated Ray in a semifinal match). Wilford also won the Wisconsin Amateur in 1937, which was the first of his four state championships, the last three of which were consecutive in 1944-1946. He won the Cuban Amateur in 1939 and the Mexican Amateur in 1941. He competed in seven U.S. Opens; he was the low amateur in 1940 and the second low amateur in 1938 and 1939. Wehrle did not have much luck in the five U.S. Amateurs in which he played; his best performance was in 1940 when he reached the semifinals. He had some bad luck in 1940 as well. He was selected for the Walker Cup team but the match was canceled because of the outbreak of World War II.

Charlie Yates (1913-2005): Charlie was raised in a home near the fourth green of Atlanta's East Lake Golf Club. He became a friend of Bob Jones and was the Secretary of the Augusta National Golf Club in his later years. Charlie won the Georgia State Amateur in 1931 and 1932, the NCAA individual title in 1934 as a Georgia Tech student, and the Western Amateur in 1935. His biggest title was the 1938 British Amateur. He played on the 1936 and 1938 Walker Cup teams, was the 1953 Walker Cup captain, and was named honorary captain in 1985. Charlie did not have much success in the U.S. Amateur. He won only eleven matches in the ten Amateurs in which he played. Like his good friend Ray Billows, Charlie was known for his sportsmanship and love of golf. In 1980 he was presented with the Bob Jones Award by the USGA.

****

Acknowledgements

I owe a debt of gratitude to Al Gore for inventing the Internet (sarcastic font and winking smiley icon omitted) and to whoever came up with the idea to digitize newspaper archives. Seriously, these two facilities make authoring a book like this 100+ years after the fact a practical venture.

Of course, it takes more than that. It takes people, and I've been blessed that some have been willing to share their time and their memories. At the top of the list is Barbara Tilles, Ray Billows' daughter. Her fond memories of her father have made this book much more than a golf account. Thanks as well to Gloria Bogle, a longtime member of Dutchess Golf Club. She and her husband Bill knew Ray and Elinor well and, by and large, Bill was the player at Dutchess to whom the torch was passed as Ray's career wound down.

Jim Peelor, the son of Jim and Winnie Peelor who were the matchmakers for Ray with both Elinor and Lynn, shared his memories. Thanks Jim. Thanks as well to Rudy Zocchi, whose microfiche-sourced compilation of newspaper articles, done 20+ years ago, remains a valuable research source, and to distinguished Vassar College English professor Bob Demaria for kindly reviewing and improving a draft of the manuscript.

Finally, thanks to Susan Wasser, Assistant Director and Curator of the USGA Museum, for her encouragement to tell this story.

About the Author

Tom Buggy is a golf historian and a past president of Dutchess Golf and Country Club in Poughkeepsie, New York. He authored the Dutchess centennial history book, *Golf's Lady of the Hudson*. His other publications include *The Golf Courses of Dutchess County*, *Dinsmore Golf Course – A Brief History*, and an article about the first six golf professionals at Dutchess that was published in *Through the Green*, the magazine of the British Golf Collectors Society.

At the time this book was written, Tom was leading a project to determine if The Edgewood Club of Tivoli is the oldest continually operated golf club in the United States. This club in Tivoli, New York was founded in 1883, primarily as a tennis club. Documented evidence of when golf was added had not yet been found.

Tom is a graduate of Villanova University. He and his wife Jackie live in Hyde Park, New York.

Index

A
Abbott, Pat 38, 56, 62, 65, 66, 98-100
Alderwood 26
Allen, Don 93
Allman, Richard 55
Armstrong, Andrew 93
Atkinson, Arthur 62
Augusta 41, 42, 52, 106

B
Baltusrol 18, 72
Bates, Eugene 80
Beechler, George 84
Benstead, H.M 42
Beverly 67
Bill, Harry 68
Billow, George 3, 12, 17, 76, 89
Billows, Ned 59, 85
Billow, Ray 3, 5, 7, 12
Billows, Ray 1, 3, 7, 8, 11, 12, 15, 17, 25, 27, 29, 31, 33, 34, 39, 46, 54-56, 60, 67, 71, 76, 78, 79, 81, 83, 84, 86, 88, 93-95, 97, 99-102, 104-107
Birkenhead, Grant 43
Bishop, Ted 65, 100
Bislinghoff, Don 85
Bogle, Bill 82
Bogle, Gloria 107
Boros, Julius 76
Brose, Charles 77
Burke, John 37, 44

C
Carnoustie 104
Carr, Joe 80
Catholic 3, 6, 48, 91

Cestone, Michael 77
Chapman, Dick 8, 10, 37, 43, 44, 51, 56, 59, 62, 65, 99, 100
Chapman, Ed 8
Ciferri, Ted 72
Coe, Charlie 77, 85, 99, 101
Colgate 24, 44
Considine, Bob 23
Corcoran, Kenny 53, 80
Creavy, Jack 10, 11, 13, 18, 57, 98
Crosby, Bing 55

D

Dawson, John 52, 99
Dear, William Jr. 55
DeCordova, Noel 52
Demaria, Bob 107
Dinsmore 100, 121
Doering, Art 45
Drexilius, Bus 24
Dudley, Ed 67
Duke of Windsor 34
Dunlap, George Jr. 18, 22, 75, 99, 101
Dunn, John Duncan 52
Dunphy, Chris 76
Dutchess 7, 12, 13, 15, 17, 19, 20, 23-25, 30, 34, 37, 43, 44, 46, 47, 52, 53, 62, 65, 71-73, 75-79, 82-85, 87-91, 97, 107, 119

E

Edgewood 109
Eisenmann, L. William 80
Ekwanok 52, 53
Evans, Chick 18, 26, 78, 104
Ewing, Cecil 35-37

F

Fiore, Fred 74
Fischer, Johnny 1, 18, 26, 55, 65, 101
Fisher, Jimmy 87
Ford, Doug 66, 71, 72
Fraser, James 72
Fruehauf, Harvey 44
Furgol, Ed 68

G

Gardner, Bob 33
Garlick, Gloria 82
Georgetown University 9, 45
Gerlin, Johnny 52
Goldman, David 99
Goodman, Johnny 1, 18, 21, 27-29, 31, 33, 35, 44-46, 56, 57, 65, 93, 94, 98, 99, 102
Goodwin, Tommy 19, 24-26, 37, 52, 54, 60, 72, 84, 87, 98
Gore, Al 107
Guenther, Paul 43

H

Haas, Fred Jr. 14, 15, 38, 98
Hagen, Walter 1, 5
Hamer, George 73, 98
Havemeyer Trophy 49
Haverstick, Harry 55
Hines, Jimmy 23
Hogan, Ben 1, 65, 68, 103
Holt, Bill Jr. 24, 25, 29, 53, 56
Homans, Eugene 99
HRGA 19, 23, 32, 33, 37, 39, 43, 51, 52, 58, 59, 71, 73, 75, 79, 83, 85
Husing, Ted 26
Hyndman, Bill 52, 72

I

International Open 31, 97
Inwood 18, 87
Ireland 26, 36

J

Jacobson, Bob 61
Jaminet, Elinor 46, 49
Jaminet, Leon and Loretta 47, 48
Johanson, Paul 84
Johnson, Paul 98
Jones, Bob 1, 3, 21, 24, 31, 33, 34, 38, 41, 42, 52, 54, 80, 95, 99, 101, 102, 104, 106

K

Keeler, O.B 1
Kelly, Roger 26, 38
Kennedy, Joseph 34
Kingston, Walter 30
Knollwood 61, 66, 74, 87
Kocsis, Charles 26, 30, 102
Korndorfer, Raymond 37
Kowal, Henry 44, 73, 79, 82
Kyle, Alex 36

L

Lakeville 14
Leonard, Thomas 74, 98
Lesley Cup 21, 22
Levinson, Johnny 38
Lincoln, Robert Todd 52, 53, 58-60, 71, 73, 75, 79, 83, 84, 97
Little, Lawson 1
Littler, Gene 83, 98
Liverpool 35
Lloyd, Lawrence 21
Lyman, Harry 77

Lynch, Arthur 59
Lowery, Eddie 8
Lyons, Jack 73

M

MacKenzie, Alister 18

Macon, A. Vernon 26

Mahnke, Helen 17

Marston, Max 111

Martin, Russell 14

Masters Tournament 9, 34, 41, 42, 51, 52, 58, 59, 71, 77, 79, 83, 97, 101-103

McCullough Jr., Duff 55, 56, 58, 98, 99, 100

McHale, James 21

McLean, Jack 99, 101

McSpaden, Jug 68

Meadowbrook 44, 49

Memphis 88-90, 100

Merion 1

Metropolis 23

Metropolitan 9, 15, 17, 18, 21-24, 33, 37, 39, 41-43, 49, 51, 52, 54, 58-60, 67, 71, 73, 75-77, 79, 83-85, 87, 97, 101, 103, 104

Millbrook 7

Minneapolis 83

Moe, Ray Jr. 84

Montclair 59

Morano, Dom 71

Morris, Art 43

Mucci, Pat 44

N

Nassau 43

NCAA 20, 44, 73, 101, 102, 104, 106

Nelson, Byron 1, 18, 30, 39, 45, 61

Nicholls, Foster 24

Nicklaus, Jack 1, 85, 101
North-South 101

O

Oakmont 37-39, 62, 104
Onondaga 65, 98
Ouimet, Francis 8, 33, 53, 99
O'Hara, Maureen 47
O'Reilly, Nan 8

P

Palmer, Arnold 1, 83
Parker, John 23
Patton, Billy Joe 52
Pebble Beach 21, 74, 102, 103
Peelor, Jim 20, 39, 47, 48, 90, 107
Pettijohn, Charles Jr. 9, 43
Picard, Henry 18
Pierce, Tommy 59, 60, 83, 09
Powelton 85
Purdy, Hal 88

Q

Quaker Ridge 17, 37
Quick, Smiley 99, 100, 107
Quilter, Raymond 35

R

Racine 1, 3-5, 12, 14, 15, 17, 25, 29, 30, 42, 44, 56, 62, 66, 89
Ramsey, Lloyd 62
Raynor, Seth 18
Reigel, Skee 99, 103
Revolta, Johnny 4, 14
Reynolds, James 71
Rhoads Hospital 68, 69

Ribner, Lloyd 87
Richardson, William 19
Ridgewood 37
Riverhill 86, 102
Roosevelt, Franklin 30
Ross, Donald 24, 43
Rozell, Ed 51, 60, 62
Runyan, Paul 18
Ruszas, Joe 67, 72, 98
Ruth, Babe 43

S

Sarazen, Gene 1, 18, 67, 88
Schappa, Bill 76
Schumacher, Don 45, 77
Shanley, Frank 25
Sheehan, Tom 44
Shields, Bill 84
Simon, Philip 21
Simpson, Wallis 34
Siwanoy 43
Smith, Jimmie 67
Smith, Horton 65
Snead, Sam 23
Somerville, Ross 38, 45, 51, 99, 103
Speno, Martin 37
Spratt, George 30, 34
Stevenson, Alex 66
Stowe, Charlie 36
Stark, William 37
Stolalik, Mike 66
Stowe, Charlie 36
Strafaci, Frank 23, 25, 26, 33, 37, 43, 51, 52, 56, 59, 71, 73, 75, 83, 85, 103
Stranahan, Frank 1, 61, 66, 77, 83, 99, 103, 105
Sweeny, Robert 75, 76

Sweetser, Jess 18-20, 22-24, 32, 33, 37, 39, 43, 53, 59, 60, 62, 63, 72-74, 97, 104
Sweet, Art 61

T

Taconic Park Commission 88
Tailer, Tommy 9, 22, 56, 59
Thom, Ken 92
Thomas, George C. 29
Thompson, Robert 26
Thomson, Jimmy 65
Thorp, Ed 8
Tilles, Barbara 4, 35, 47, 48, 67, 71, 74, 86, 93, 107
Tillinghast, A.W. 17
Woods, Tiger 91
Travers, Jerome 65
Travis, Walter 52, 104
Trevor, George 1, 7, 11
Trier, Clara 3, 6, 17, 90, 91
Troon 33, 35
Truman, Harry 36
Tucker, Jack 19
Turnesa, Willie 1, 10, 18, 37, 38, 44, 51-53, 55, 56, 62, 65, 77, 78, 80, 88, 89, 94, 98-100, 104, 105

U

Urzetta, Sam 83, 99, 104, 105
USGA 26, 33, 36, 65, 68, 78, 79, 93, 97, 104, 106, 107

V

Vallo, Joe 20
VanBenschoten, Lynn 90
VanBenschoten, Wes 24, 37, 76, 77
Vardon, Harry 80
Vassar College 30, 107
Vaughn, Ed 76

Villanova Iniversity 109
Voigt, George 9, 22
Von Elm, George 33

W

Wadewitz, Edward 5, 6, 42, 62
Wadsworth, Gene 75
Walker, George Herbert 35
Ward, Marvin Bud 1, 19, 24, 27, 38, 45, 46, 49, 54-56, 61, 62, 65, 66, 77, 80, 93, 94, 98-100, 102, 105
Ward, Dudley 19
Ward, John 80
Wasser, Susan 107
Watson, Tom 1
Wehrle, Wilford 4, 25, 29, 30, 33, 44, 49, 54, 56, 65, 66, 105
Wellesley College 46
Westland, Jack 99
White, Paul 62
White, Ronnie 80
Whitehead, Charles 21, 67
Whitman Publishing Company 5
Wiggins, Roy 26
Winged Foot 8-12, 17, 19, 20, 22, 24, 25, 34, 37, 40, 51, 54, 55, 61, 72, 75, 76, 80, 84, 93, 94, 98, 100
Winter, Alpheus 37
Wolcott, W.K. 14
Wood, Craig 18, 54

Y

Yahnundasis 68, 70, 72
Yale 104
Yankees 67

Z

Zimmerman, Arnold 53
Zocchi, Rudy 107

Font Usage: Main Text: Janson TextW01-55Roman, 12-point.

Lightning Source UK Ltd.
Milton Keynes UK
UKHW021822160223
417092UK00004B/474